Brian Wright was educ
Christ Church, Oxfor
Literature before goin
period as a teacher, he went into acting and has remained in the profession ever since, as well as writing, directing and script editing for television. At present he is script editor of the BBC 1 Classic Series

Apart from plays and revue material he has published a children's story, *The Canal Children*, and is now at work on a novel. *Penge Papers*, originally written for radio and broadcast in a series of readings by the author on Radio 3, attracted an enormous response from critics and general public alike.

Brian Wright

Penge Papers

Confessions of an Unwaged Metropolitan Househusband

Pan Books
London and Sydney

First published 1985 by Souvenir Press Ltd
This edition published 1986 by Pan Books Ltd,
Cavaye Place, London SW10 9PG
9 8 7 6 5 4 3 2 1

ISBN 0 330 29506 3
Printed in Great Britain by
Collins, Glasgow

Contents

To Big Roob, El Fid, Banana Chaw, Soapy and the Plonkers, not forgetting Est and Henna Huss.

'. . . Philosopher, sir?'

'An observer of human nature, sir,' said Mr Pickwick.

'Ah, so am I. Most people are when they've little to do and less to get . . .'

Charles Dickens, *The Pickwick Papers*

Prologue

These confessions were originally confided to a microphone and three bemused staff at Broadcasting House. Later they were transmitted on Radio Three, during the intervals of several rather demanding concerts. Please don't ask me why. It might have been intended as a pat on the back; equally, it could have been a punishment. On Radio Three, now I come to think of it, it could well have been both. I only know I was surprised to receive a flow of letters from listeners. I hadn't bargained on any listeners—certainly not responsive ones.

Most of them had never been to Penge, of course. All of them had obviously heard that it was some kind of national joke; yet somehow, nearly all of them seemed to identify with the place. Intimately. This unnerved me, I must admit. I began to be haunted by the idea that I was describing a state of mind rather than a suburb; that somewhere, in the darkness of Penge railway tunnel or along the grassy embankments approaching Beckenham Junction, there was—unknown to commuters—a secret frontier, across which consenting English adults occasionally stumbled during bouts of boredom, daydream or dyspepsia. In short, that Penge belonged on the same map as Grantchester, Coronation Street or Camelot. On the farthest edge of it, no doubt—the other side of Pook's Hill and down a bit to the left; way beyond East Cheam; half-way to Queer Street.

Simple common sense will tell you that Penge is six

miles south of Piccadilly Circus—as the crow flies, that is, although it's not a trip crows make much nowadays. In fact, they could have cancelled flights a hundred and thirty years ago. Nobody seems to have noticed, but Penge has been visible for miles around since the Crystal Palace was shunted across from Hyde Park and re-erected at the highest point of the parish. When the Palace burned down in 1936, the BBC thoughtfully supplied a television mast by way of compensation. They took the precaution of waiting until the Luftwaffe had gone out of business, of course.

I suppose Sydenham and Anerley have an equal claim to Paxton's giant greenhouse, and to the Beeb's slim-line phallus; but the mast stands up four-square over the High Street, and we surely belong to each other. On clear days, junior typists in Acton office blocks stare out of windows and scream, 'Oh look, the Eiffel Tower,' unaware that cast-iron exhibitionism came to Penge a full fifteen years before it reached Paris. Every now and then I shock gullible visitors by casually mentioning that —on a good day—you can see France from Penge. They squint between the chimney stacks, half-convinced by their own ignorance . . . Incidentally, you will notice that the aviation warning lights on the aerial have developed a permanent neurotic twitch, as though the tower realised it marked a spot the rest of the nation finds ridiculous, and took the matter personally.

Penge people are very sensitive on this point. They know, from bitter experience, that to admit residence here guarantees a snigger, almost anywhere that English is spoken. A useful gambit along the cocktail belt, perhaps, but a serious handicap to upwardly mobile Pengeians. Many of them pretend to be domiciled in Sydenham, Bromley or Dulwich, depending on whether they wish to appear a cut or two above or a cut or two below. And they spend all their free time frantically looking for somewhere else they can afford to live. To be fair, I expect they're just as sensitive in Wigan, Neasden and Potters Bar. Funnily enough, they're not bothered so much in Catford; they enjoy the challenge, I think, and of course, they're tough over there; the greyhound stadium makes a big difference, too. Punters dying the death on your doorstep twice a week—bound to make you more philosophical.

Personally, I like living in a comic ghetto. I feel I'm in touch with something mysterious, profound, beyond myself. For me, Wigan and Penge are holy places: Glastonbury and Lindisfarne, smothered in custard pie. Why certain towns should be singled out for national ridicule is a very deep question—and therefore beyond me. My friend Reg says it's just another example of the innate class-ridden structure of English society. But he says that about everything, from Christmas to liquorice all-sorts. Mind you, most self-respecting, owner-occupying Pengeians do consider themselves—against all the odds—to be, well, a smidgeon genteel. After all, we're practically Home Counties out here, where the south-east rump of London feels the north-west knee of Kent. I've actually heard the name pronounced the French way for effect. Penge—Ponge. We live in Ponge. But then, Pissarro painted a picture of Penge West station and it's hanging in the Courtauld Institute, so anything is possible—anything. The publication of these confessions is final proof of that.

Greetings from Penge. Wish you were here, and so on. But then again, you already are—or soon will be; in spirit at least.

1 *The Call*

Fulfilled, that's me; a complete man. People can hear it in my voice, I think; see it in my face, the way I walk. Seriously, it shows. I wish I had a fiver each time someone said to me, 'You look different, you've changed'. I tell them, 'I'm fulfilled'. 'Oh yes?' they say, looking elsewhere, rather cool. You know, as if my zip was undone. I suppose it's not the sort of thing you admit to any more, not where I live; not in Penge. Not unless you're one of those who knock on doors and say it to total strangers, or shout it down a megaphone—up the High Street, under a banner, on a wet Saturday afternoon: 'Brothers and sisters, I am fulfilled.'

My point is that fulfilment doesn't drop like manna nowadays, not in Penge. If it did, the borough cleansing department would shovel it up prompt and dump it somewhere. Don't get me wrong. When I say fulfilment I'm not talking about—you know—the pleasures of the flesh, that old-fashioned, permissive 'sixties stuff. Nor am I talking about happiness, football pools for the soul—five billion to one you'll never come up. What I'm on about is my place in society, what my friend Reg likes to call the social nexus. That's where I'm fulfilled. Complete, as I say. Mark you, I can't take any credit for it; I didn't set out to be fulfilled. I'm not an idealist, a radical, a romantic, a fanatic, a guru, or an anything in particular. I don't even watch *Songs of Praise* after tea on Sunday, or take the *Guardian* regularly. I'm just your average suburban husband and father who could have been Robert Redford, given the right breaks.

It took me ten years, and three different difficult schools, to decide that I didn't like teaching English. To be honest, I decided within a couple of days, but it took me ten years to decide to do anything about my decision. My friend Reg—he *says* he's my friend—tells me I'm feckless. 'You're feckless,' he says. 'Socially and politically feckless.' Well, there it is; if you lack feck, you lack feck. One-legged men win very few medals at the marathon.

Nevertheless, by way of a decision, or pending a decision, I finally applied to my education authority for a year's paid leave to do a higher degree—what's known as a sabbatical, which sounds rather pious, but my subject was purely secular: 'An approach to English Pornography, with special reference to the poems of Lord Rochester'. I thought this might lead to some interesting new openings, in higher education, I mean. (I say higher, but anything above basement level would have suited me down to the ground.)

My application for paid leave was refused; this, you see, was 1980, a bad year for mendicant scholars. I was in no mood to be put off by municipal philistines, however, not after a decade clinging to the chalk-face. My wife's warnings couldn't stop me, nor friend Reg's sensible advice. (I always ignore sensible advice, on principle.) Everyone has a right to dignified failure, in my opinion; show me anybody who ever learned anything, or was improved, by success. You'd think the British would understand that: Charge of the Light Brigade, Captain Scott, Dunkirk, Concorde, the Commonwealth, Social Democracy—we specialise in interesting, instructive cock-ups. Then we go and ruin them by pretending they're triumphs. But not me, not guilty. I gave up my job, began work on my thesis; a literary entrepreneur, my own two feet—all that.

A year later I was still gathering material. Well, it's a big subject, pornography. After another year, I'd written five thousand words and collected an album of remarkable illustrations. I'd also diversified into fiction: a series of promising prose poems to my bank manager who, it turned out, had no ear for poetry. I thought that in the depths of a trade recession I deserved some credit for my vision and courage, but a prophet is not only without honour in his own country, he's permanently stuck for cash. And in his own family, I tell you, he's the original alligator in the toilet bowl. My wife threatened to leave; my two daughters actually went—only as far as Orpington, but at four and five years old, with 20p in your pocket and leaky wellingtons, that's desperation. I may be feckless, but I'm sensitive with it. I began to apply for teaching jobs again.

Now you'd have thought, wouldn't you, that half a doctorate in philosophy was better than none? Not a bit of it, far worse. 'PhD? PhD?'—headmasters *sniffed*, as if it was a brand of cheap bottled sauce; my subject matter wasn't much to their taste, either. But the fact is, schools aren't into teachers at the moment, there isn't the call for them. It's something to do with falling rolls, which sounds like a limousine going over a cliff, or a catastrophe in a sandwich bar, but what it comes down to is a low conception rate in the late 'sixties and 'seventies. All those permissive swingers, too bloody clever by half. I probably couldn't get a teaching job today if I was a combination of R.A. Butler, Mr Chips and the Princess of Wales. A couple of power strikes and a television blackout this winter, things could change, but for the moment, the Department of Health and Social Security is signing up teachers like there was no tomorrow. According to my friend Reg there won't be, of course—no more rolls left to fall. Reg won't ever be fulfilled, that's for certain; it would deprive him of his greatest pleasure, looking on the black side.

In the 'sixties, when anyone cast doubts on my schemes to become rich and famous, I used to shrug and say, 'I can always teach.' In the 'seventies, when anyone criticised my plan to go round the world and write a book about it, I used to shrug and say, 'I can always go on the dole.' In the 'eighties, when I really had to, I just shrugged. And shrugged—like I was shell-shocked. My degree, my thirteen GCEs, my eleven plus and my extramural piano lessons blew up behind me. Crumm . . . ! But at Catford Labour Exchange I was in amongst the walking wounded. *That* forced you to face some of the great, unanswered questions of twentieth-century society: 'Why can't we go abroad for a holiday next year?' 'Why can't our kids have a home computer?' and, 'Who is going to pay for the roof to be mended?' Reg has long, irrelevant answers to all these, of course, but this itself poses the central question of our age: why Reg? And if so, how come he's a rep with the Gas Board in Lewisham?

Anyway, in the event, I was very soon back in full-time, if not gainful, employment. My wife returned to her old job as manager of a photographic studio and appointed me cook-housekeeper-nanny, all found and living in. The girls were appalled—my track record in this field is not good—but I think it means she still loves me. Even if she doesn't, the net result is the same, for without her initiative, I'd never have discovered my true vocation.

To anticipate objections from the six pints a night, jockstrap and snooker brigade, my role-swapping was only incidental.

'Aren't you ashamed?' they say. 'Demeaned, embarrassed?'

'Is the cossack ashamed of his horse?' I ask. 'Is the captain demeaned by his ship, the pole vaulter embarrassed by his pole?'

They smirk and their eyebrows dance innuendoes.

'We househusbands are free to be real men, not macho marionettes!' I yell, waving my string shopping bag angrily.

In fact, believe it or not, my Damascus Road was a trip to Sainsbury's—Bromley branch. Inside to the left, by the offal freezer, that's where it happened, the blinding light . . . I was riffling through the pigs' kidneys on behalf of the cats, when I heard this . . . this Voice. A very clear, distinct Voice. It said, it said:

'They're bits and pieces of animals, darling—cows and sheep and things. They don't mind because they're dead and they expect it. Lots of animals eat other animals. You remember? Lin Chow brought a mouse through the cat door.'

The Voice came from under some bobbed auburn hair, on top of a yellow jump-suit. A youngish face. But the voice was ageless; more a tradition than a voice, really.

'Come and find those biscuits Daddy likes,' it went on. 'They're called Garibaldi because General Garibaldi invented them. He was a soldier, like Uncle Jeremy. But not British.'

The Voice was talking to a *baby*, perched on her shopping trolley. He couldn't understand a word, not a word; wasn't interested. But he was trapped, stuck there, facing this *Blue Peter* commissar, this walking, talking, *Readers' Digest* Cindy Doll his parent had turned into. Mother Jekyll and Sister Hyde. He just sat there, but you could see the thought developing, behind those glazed baby eyes: roll on teenage—and Revenge.

She shoved on through pastries, tinned meats, frozen fish and fruit and veg. Continuous running commentary, in full stereo—she couldn't have projected more if she'd been doing a double-act at the Albert Hall.

'Look, darling, this side says grams and this side says pounds.' The child was too young to be embarrassed, or he'd have died on the spot, slumped across the economy-size Persil . . .

The Voice wasn't the first of its kind I'd heard, of course. You meet these lecturing, hectoring, complacent parents all over; south of Birmingham especially. They usually drive automatic continental estates with tow-bars attached, and big smelly dogs inside. Reg, being Reg, reckons they're engaged in a tribal ritual, signifying membership of a verbalising power elite—or something. Whatever label you stuck on her, the Voice was a prize specimen; she even kept her monologue going through the check-out. I had to admire that: packing groceries in a supermarket sends me all of a Jack Lemmon.

I abandoned my trolley by ladies' toiletries and trailed the Voice out to the car-park, curious to know if she ever stopped . . . There was a Peugeot estate. With tow-bar. And a large basset hound peering through the wind-screen. But she stopped talking to the kid and started on me instead.

'Haven't you got anything better to do than gawp at other people?'

'Since you mention it, no,' I said.

'Go away or I'll call a policeman.'

'Call him what?' I asked, winking at the boy. He began to cry, obviously unused to communication.

'Yes, darling, he *is* a silly man isn't he?'

I went back to my trolley. Yet, in a sense, there was no going back ever again. I stood, staring down at the frozen pigs' kidneys, giving off waves, like an infra-red photograph—me, not the kidneys. Because, you see, I meant what I told the Voice; that came straight from the heart. I *had* nothing better to do, absolutely nothing. Suddenly, for the first time, I understood—something I'd known all my life, really: watching people is what I'm good at; I never get tired of it; I'm one of the world's observers. That's what I'm meant for, basically all I ever wanted. Fulfilment, you see?

I won't pretend my wife shared this revelation, exactly. And my daughters, well, they treat me like I'm mental anyway—it's a phase they're going through. As for Reg:

'Dole hysteria,' he says.

'What do they know of England who only the work place know?' I ask.

'You've succumbed to the chronic voyeurism of Western civilisation,' he says.

'Was the Venerable Bede a voyeur?' I cry. 'Were Cobbett, Mayhew, Marx and Engels, Masters and Johnson?'

'They were activists, utilising available organs of communication,' he explains.

I hate to admit it, but if these memoirs have an 'onlie begetter', it's got to be Reg, the comrade from the Gas Board.

Whenever you're in Penge—unlikely I realise—but if ever, watch out for me. I'm the one watching you.

2 *Neighbours*

New neighbours have moved in, next door. Geographically speaking, our only neighbours in the avenue, because we're end-of-terrace, you see—these distinctions count for something in Penge. I'm told, those three yards of patchy tarmacadam and two inches of rotting fence, they put a couple of thousand on the value of the house—at a cost: our hall, bathroom and loo must be ten times colder than anyone else's, and allergic to fungus. My statistic is only an estimate, of course; I've never penetrated as far as a neighbour's bathroom or loo to check. Typical English bourgeois, says my friend Reg. I tell him, the Englishman's home, etcetera. Exactly, he says. We're terrified of being snubbed, i.e. snobbed.

He's knocking on a bit, is Reg. He loves to regale me with stories of his boyhood in the Far East—West Ham, I mean, behind the football ground. Merry cockney tenants out on their doorsteps, chai-iking, gossiping, peeling spuds, shelling peas, mixing batter. It wouldn't work on the avenue, now, I know that; you'd have to run extension leads for the electric mixers, the noise would be deafening. Besides, you can't see some of the doorsteps for tastefully arranged shrubs and creepers. It's gone, all that, along with mutton broth, chamber-pots and the music-hall. The unemployment boom could start a revival, I suppose—some folk-lorique Freddy Laker will cash in—but it would never do for up-town Penge; unemployment keeps a low profile here. Along the avenue I'm the only ratepayer in his prime who has 'come out', as it were. Judging from the strange glances I get when I wave my wife off to work or potter down to the shops, the term is pretty near the mark.

Maybe that colours my judgement, and these new neighbours may prove me wrong, but I must confess, the word 'neighbour' doesn't have much to do with neighbourliness hereabouts—barring a kind of tabloid curiosity, a vague stirring when the ambulance or hearse rolls up. People are 'neighbourly' the way they're 'C of E' on official forms. The old faith lingers, like the annual lump in the throat when you hear 'Once in Royal David's City', but that's all. There's an elderly lady a few doors down with whom I exchange commonplaces that sound quite liturgical, in fact:

'What a lovely day!'

'Ah yes, indeed.'

'Miserable, isn't it?'

'Mm, miserable.'

'Much better today.'

'Oh, much better . . .'

Three months ago I saw a van—or was it an ambulance?—whatever it was, it carted her husband away. Nobody seems to know why or where, or like to ask now.

'Morning, husband settling down all right in hospital/funny farm/the nick/Kingdom Come?'

'Yes, isn't it a lovely day?'

A couple of pints and Reg will water your beer describing how much better they handled these things in the East End during the war. I sometimes think Reg's idea of Utopia is a public air-raid shelter full of cheerful families making cups of tea and having jolly sing-songs. It may come to pass yet, but I take his point: a heavy fall of snow or a flooded drain and commuter *gemütlichkeit* bucks up a treat; out come the shovels, squeegees, buckets, brooms and mops, even wheelbarrows. The avenue wears its waggon-train look, and everybody walks like John Wayne, ladies included. Till Nature's shoved back out of sight where it belongs and we can relax again and forget we're human. Once someone's cat got stuck up a tree, and the fire brigade was called. Pots of tea appeared for the officers, and civilians came outside to join them, dunking biscuits and watching the rescue. Didn't do the cat much good, but everybody else had great fun. At the finish we all stood up and applauded. I've tried chasing our cats up trees in the hope of a repeat performance, but they're unco-operative animals at the best of times.

Down the avenue long-established residents operate a rigid seniority system. They only talk to those who have lived here for a minimum of fifteen years. We barely muster eight. Maybe they just don't want to know people who live in places like this; maybe they haven't got over the Second World War yet: careless talk costs lives—the chief watch-dogs of the system date back that far. Two of them are married to each other. She's a scrawny little woman with a cast-iron perm and a screw-top mouth, on which she paints crimson Shirley Temple lips. Her glance sucks you in and spits you out in one quick action; I think she must have had a nasty experience in the black-out. The experience might have been her husband. He's built like a St Bernard; he walks like a St Bernard; he looks like a St Bernard, a hairless St Bernard—a brandy-less St Bernard, unfortunately.

Three times a day the St Bernard drags an ancient golden retriever round the park where it defecates prodigiously, in forbidden places contrary to the bye-laws. This seems to give them both great satisfaction, which is nice, because neither of them seems to do anything else much. He harangues the chosen few about their cars occasionally, miming the action of BL components with fingers the colour and shape of German sausages. Which reminds me: he did speak to me once. I was washing our old Mini-traveller when he and the dog returned from their bowel movements.

'Nice day for it,' I said.

'You got trouble there,' he replied, looking at the car. To emphasise the point, the dog urinated up against the passenger door.

Being about as mechanically minded as a Barbara Cartland heroine, I've been expecting disaster ever since. Perhaps, if we survive in the avenue long enough to beat the fifteen year embargo, he'll amplify that remark. The state of our finances, we'll still be jump-starting the Mini every morning.

Our new neighbours next door have a new Citroën *and* a new Mini—and three newish children. He's a short, plump traveller in pharmaceuticals: 'I see, a legal drug pusher,' I said, but he didn't laugh. His wife is tall and pear-shaped, an ex-social worker. She's taken to motherhood the way nuns take to the veil: flat shoes, straight skirts, cardigans and head-scarves—a faint look of the Royals at a point-to-point. When I told her I was a full-time voluntary observer of human nature, the resemblance became quite marked. Without doubt they're what I call short-term transients. By short-term I mean about five years; by transients I mean middle-class fugitives from the inner city, or aspiring middle-class—or perspiring, as the case may be. Penge is a recognised staging-post on the great escape route, the Grand Canyon of South London. Only the most resolute make it to the lush interior beyond: Beckenham, Chislehurst, Farnborough—and Edenbridge, of course, the commercial man's Beverly Hills.

These greenhorns next door look as if they'll make it

eventually. What sort of neighbours they'll make before they hit the trail again isn't altogether clear; a quick check on the pantechnicon when they first arrived was inconclusive. I had to pretend there was something wrong with the car and take a closer look. (Well, there *is* something wrong with the car—I had to pretend I knew what it was.) A professional observer's interest you understand, nothing personal. There are few sights more likely to make you feel the general futility of human existence than a furniture van being emptied by removal men in a hurry—all those kitchen chairs, stained beds and rickety night tables, naked on the pavement. There ought to be a law, domestic exposure. Anyhow, the newcomers go in for a discreet blend of sub-Heal's classic, Habitaterie and Japanese micro-chipaware. Their exact classification is going to take time. I'd better explain.

Along the avenue neighbours are best classified by the style of architecture they favour. The most popular is California Regency Rural: painted façades, bottle-glass windows, patio doors, brass knockers, fake coach-lamps, and so on—a poor man's version of the sort of house actors are supposed to live in, according to photos in *TV Times*. Secondly, there is the more up-market Scandinavian Maison Manorial: white walls, stripped pine, storm shutters, wrought-iron work, landscaped back yards—that sort of thing. The degree of conversion to either of these styles determines the rate at which the property increases in value; and this, of course, is crucial in deciding the next stage of the great escape, be it to Beckenham, Chislehurst, Farnborough or Edenbridge. I'm convinced the glamorous widow down the road actually chooses her lovers—amongst other things—for their skills at home improvement. One was a dab-hand at door-hanging, another a compulsive decorator, a third an intrepid roofer. Broad, bronzed young men, they tend to cohabit for about six months; and in three busy years the glamorous widow has made herself the queen of the California Regency Rurals. Beckenham must beckon by now, if not Chislehurst. And whoever buys that house will inhabit more than bricks and mortar: every door-frame tells a story, every tile, every inch of tongue and grooving.

The avenue, by the way, consists of four terraces of three up, three down Edwardian clerks' dwellings. If you inspect the few still occupied by the very old, the hard-up, the incompetent or the uncompetitive, you can still see that's all they are. In fact, this creates a third distinctive style: Festival of Britain Dilapidated. I'm afraid we belong to it—with a slight list towards Scandinavian Maison Manorial. The terraces were thrown up by a smart operator when the railways finally punched holes through London's southern hills, and the city penpushers began to colonise. He built several streets of them, in ascending order of size and superiority. The avenue is at the lowest end of the scale; but most residents would argue it's very near the top—in tone. A nice tone, they say, worth keeping up. By 'tone', I think they mean a precise mathematical quotient, reached by dividing the number of houses by the number of teenagers, council tenants, new Commonwealth residents, undecorated exteriors and unweeded gardens.

This explains a curious behaviour pattern I've observed amongst active male householders around breakfast time. Leaving for work, the subject moves slowly from door to front gate, scanning for evidence of depredations by vandals, greenfly, dogs, slugs and late-night addicts of McDonald's and Kentucky Fried. Fastidious unlatching and latching of gate is followed by a whip-pan up to the eaves, probing for subsidence, wood-warp and flaky paintwork. Subject then accelerates away with an admiring tracking shot of his tight, right little investment. It's a running check on the tone quotient, obviously. When *I* sally forth from hearth and home, I carefully look the other way, to avoid paying bills in imagination I can't afford in fact.

A mature Festival of Britain Dilapidated style is only achieved by consistent artistic neglect. I don't think the neighbours appreciate this. Going by the pained looks I get from some of them, they see me as a threat to residential tone. Nothing has been said, of course, but as I was paying the milkman last week, the four-year-old heir to a California Regency Rural household accosted me.

'When are you going to paint your house?' he said.

I was so shaken that when I went to clip him round the ear I missed. Afterwards Reg came up with a whole glossary of acid comments I could have made but didn't. Things like: 'Tell your pillock of a father it will take more than a coat of paint to cover up the inevitable decline of capitalism.' In my opinion a clip round the ear would have been much more succinct. But you see the lengths the avenue is prepared to go in defence of its values? I fear this kindergarten brownshirt was sent in to soften me up for some kind of heavy mob later on.

Which makes it all the more vital to classify these new neighbours. They inherited a superb example of Festival of Britain Dilapidated. When I came back from collecting the child allowances yesterday, a skip had appeared outside. Today a transit van arrived with a squad of lively young builders. They began banging away in the middle of the house, and filling the skip with chunks of Festival of Britain Dilapidated. Later, assorted bags of building stuff and a pile of sand were delivered. Later still, the dedicated pear-shaped mother came round, to ask whether some patio doors could be carried behind the terrace and across my garden—and was I aware my back extension gutter needed replacing?. She looks pure Scandinavian Maison Manorial, but the evidence says otherwise. Our new neighbours could be militant recruits to California Regency Rural—I just don't know. Maybe Penge is becoming too hot for me.

3 *Egnep*

Now I'm an unemployed teacher I spend a lot of time in Egnep. Egnep: that's Penge spelled backwards, what I call the other Penge, the hidden Penge, the one the visitor or unobservant native never sees. Ranks of terraces flanked by files of parked cars, that's Penge; motorised, disciplined, domestic units. Egnep is the *terra incognita* beyond, the strange, uncharted territory glimpsed through back windows, north, south, east or west, as far as the back windows of the next terrace; a world apart, delights and terrors round every shrub, shed or herbaceous border . . . Six gardens along from us there's a greenhouse overflowing with illegal botanic substances; next door but one they've somehow kept their Anderson air-raid shelter for twenty-five years, complete with emergency stocks of tinned milk and bully beef; next door but two, at the bottom of the garden, there's a tableau of polystyrene fairies, in very compromising positions . . . And the people went out from Penge and dwelt in the wilderness of Egnep, and made of it their very own and secret kingdom.

The Egnepese are closely related to Pengeians, of course, but their language, customs and dress are quite distinct. A suit and tie, for example, that's a rare sight in Egnep. Nine sightings out of ten are accounted for by aliens: estate agents, surveyors, council wallahs and the like. By the same token, Penge rarely sees the muddy wellies, stained trousers, grimy headgear, assorted sportswear, swimwear and degrees of nakedness that make up the picturesque native costume of Egnep. The language tends towards the picturesque, too; Egnepese is rich and colourful, the product of a hundred years' continuous struggle (against busted lawnmowers, marauding cats, diabolic kids and endemic greenfly). You see and hear things in Egnep that can't be seen or heard anywhere else, apart from adult movies or desperate fringe theatre.

In fact, the deeper you penetrate into Egnep the more private, uninhibited and taboo-free behaviour becomes. Those rows and rows of front porches in Penge are frontier guard posts, a thin blue line of respectability. Once across the border, you're in sovereign Egnep territory, and anything goes . . . This might explain the current fashion for unalarming burglar alarms; they're a status symbol down the avenue just now. They jangle away nightly, so regularly, nobody seems to notice any more—except the insurance agents, of course. Certainly not the burglars; they come and go across the Egnep frontier more or less unmolested—Penge Pimpernels.

My friend Reg can't be doing with these fantasies. He says they obscure the nature of the capitalist conspiracy, the great privatising, home-owning threat to communal utopia. Reg is an Egnephobe, definitely. If he had his way Egnep would be common land; every garden fence down, every shrub and herbaceous border nationalised. I try to tell him: his politics amount to sacrilege in England; privacy is the national religion, and Anglo-Saxons will rob, rape and pillage for their faith. In his heart of hearts Reg must know that. You should hear him drool on about his old mum's front room, back in West Ham, when Hitler was chucking buzz-bombs across the Channel. A sacred place, that front room, consecrated to

Christmas, Easter, funerals, weddings and serious courtship—that is, licensed heavy petting. A chapel of privacy was the old prole parlour. The polished linoleum, the starched antimacassars and sideboard runners; the grim plunk of the wooden clock on the mantelpiece, the grin of the china dogs guarding it; old Reg treasures them all. He's worshipped at the shrine of privacy, even Red Reg. Egnep rules. Viva Egnep.

It's not really a single, sovereign state, of course, but a collection of tiny tribal fiefdoms, united by their common purpose—privacy. And as far as its liege lord is concerned, each of these tribal domains is unique. At weekends, in favourable weather, you can see proud owner-occupiers taking carefully selected aliens on guided tours, solemnly inspecting very ordinary flower-beds, vegetable patches, sheds and other unremarkable features. Every home is a stately home in Egnep; they never seem to tire of this Lilliput patriotism. I'm afraid it's a tradition I can't warm to myself. *Our* visitors are given strict instructions *not* to look at the teeming imperfections round the place, and to ignore the garden completely—I always do. Penge clay is a sod to dig, so to speak. Our garden is virgin Egnep: convenient summer pasture for the kids, good forage for starlings and thrushes, and excellent cover for my researches into the local tribes and their relentless pursuit of privacy.

They seldom find it, that's the funny part, and when they do it's more apparent than real. Illusion, not reality—what else could they expect? Fiefdom upon tiny fiefdom, packed together like After Eight mints; what you can't see you can hear, and what you can't hear—over fences, round shrubs, through walls—you can guess. For instance, I can tell by the vocal range, technique and repertoire of the elderly single lady next door that she used to sing soprano lead in amateur musicals. My Nelson Eddy impersonation is guaranteed to shut her up in mid-quaver . . . 'Oh Rose Marie I love you . . .' And then there's the window cleaner hazard. Have you ever noticed? They always appear at moments of crisis—like ravens—when the washing machine floods, or you're picking your nose, or changing the baby. Privacy is not so easily come by, in Egnep *or* Penge—or Timbuctoo, for that matter.

Look at the glamorous widow down the road—everybody does, she'd obviously be heartbroken if they didn't. And everybody knows she sunbathes in the altogether: indoors under a sun-lamp, outdoors on the pastel-tinted patio; screened left and right by wattle fences, rhododendron and wistaria. But, indoors or out, well within view of the retired railwayman's binoculars at the back of the terrace opposite. He took to inviting sceptical friends round to prove his viewpoint, and they carried the good news out into Penge—I believe it for one. The all-year-round mottled pig-skin tan the widow sports is powerful circumstantial evidence. And on hot days I've noticed neighbouring Egnep men somehow find urgent jobs to do up ladders, or at the bottom of gardens. Last summer, to my certain knowledge, there were two broken legs and one case of concussion.

Does the glamorous widow know, I wonder? Does she, or anyone, really care? The Victorians and Edwardians left or planted great screens of trees in Egnep. They had more to hide perhaps, felt guiltier, any rate. But trees were one of Egnep's glories: copper-beech, poplar, cypress, laburnum, giant cherry; merrie England in miniature. Mostly lopped or felled now, for the sake of longer, greener lawns, straighter, neater flower-beds, another yard of sunlight. Maybe the privacy of the ostrich is all that's required in Egnep nowadays, a bit of space to pretend.

Take Fred and Freda. I don't know their real names, I've never met them, but Fred and Freda is what I call the occupants of the bijou end-of-terrace house on our starboard stern. I sometimes think their lives are more familiar than my own. From my daughter's bedroom you can see the custom-built country-style kitchen gleaming through what they call—appropriately—a picture window. At night the eye-level grill shines across Egnep like the Green Eye of the Little Yellow God; the William Morris sun blinds are never drawn, nor in the conservatory extension; you can look beyond the potted plants and wicker-work to a reproduction country chintz interior. The floor above is similarly open for inspection, comprising a deep pink boudoir place, and a view of Japanese prints and a gilded lamp on the landing. The bathroom window is frosted over. Enough is enough, even for Fred and Freda.

Their house reminds me of those cross-sectional models you find in museums, or a cabinet in the twilight room at London Zoo—especially during one of their frequent parties. Three dozen bright, wavering creatures flitting in and out, back and forth, up and down; lights behind the frosted glass flicking on and off, off and on. It's the catch-22 of Egnep, you see: once you've achieved the comfortable, prosperous private life every Englishman craves, you can only signal your success by somehow going public . . .

Fred and Freda's quarrels are a regular Egnep entertainment. Four- and six-letter words carry farther than the others—have you ever noticed? The show usually starts in the kitchen, mixes across to the conservatory, fades amongst the potted plants, and dissolves in the country-chintz interior, where there's an interval. The second act begins on the landing, cuts to the boudoir place, and ends with a bewildering *son-et-*

lumière behind the frosted glass, in the best tradition of the cliff-hanger.

Of course, my friend Reg blames it all on conspicuous consumption, the tyranny of the market: privacy means property and property means putting your mouth where your money is. (Reg is full of these phrases, he collects them in a little red notebook.) I think he pines for the old backyard: the mangle, the rabbit hutches, pigeon lofts, chicken runs, chopping blocks, coal-sheds, outside lavs and zinc baths hanging on a rusty nail. But I've got to admit, these days the Egnep wilderness is up for grabs. It is written: thou shalt not covet thy neighbour's wife—nobody mentioned his electric lawnmower. It seems grass isn't grass any more without it's trimmed by the national grid; property isn't property unless it's patrolled by one of these hungry metal herbivores. If privacy includes the right to silence, then don't live down our street between April and September; with mains clippers barbering the hedges, masonry drills gouging away like electronic woodpeckers, the pits at Brand's Hatch would be more peaceful. I've taken to wearing one of these Walkman cassettes round the house. I've taped two hours of silence on it. I stuck the microphone down the cellar in a jar of cotton wool.

And the exploitation doesn't stop at consumer durables. Whatever happened to the old 'No Hawkers and Circulars' routine? Every day they're at it, Messrs Bumf and Hype, buttonholing you from breakfast to bedtime. Leaflets, brochures, adverts, via letterbox, press or cathode ray. And insidious telephone calls: personal calls from brisk young girls who know my name and attempt to seduce me with patio doors, or aluminium windows, or swimming pools, or ornamental paving. Unwaged, bone-idle and disenchanted, I'm beyond temptation, but I can see Egnep being colonised by Penge in the finish, just as surely as Coca-Cola conquered Mexico. The frontier will vanish, Egnep will be swallowed up entirely. Gazing out across the back garden one night last week, I saw this mysterious light moving hither and yon. Closer and closer it came. I stood there transfixed, expecting some supernatural or extraterrestrial encounter. But it was more shocking than that: a thin, teenage policeman loomed up outside the kitchen window—a bona fide, accredited Penge officer—wandering about where his writ does not run! He said someone had reported a prowler; I daresay Cecil Rhodes said the same thing about Matabeleland.

The Egnepese will never surrender completely, I suppose. They'll continue to guard their privacy long after it's gone, just as they do now. We have three tribal wars in progress this very minute, border disputes basically . . . The glamorous widow protested about the encroachment of her neighbour's bindweed; he ignored her, so she instructed current boyfriend to spray neighbour's garden with weed-killer—unfortunately it accidentally poisoned the tortoise, and neighbour retaliated by hosing her shrubs with powerful defoliant. The dispute has now escalated into an action for damages . . . Fred and Freda recently offended the retired railwayman, lighting a bonfire on washing day, and besmirching his long engine driver's underwear. He counter-attacked on *their* washing day, and they rather foolishly struck back again on *his*. He then made a pre-emptive strike, burning oily old rags intermittently for a fortnight. Fred and Freda have made a strategic withdrawal to the launderette.

They were already in trouble with my musical comedy neighbour: her cats have appropriated their garden as a private litter tray. Musical comedy lady refuses to hear ill of cats under any circumstances, so Fred and Freda took to shovelling firm evidence across her fence after dark. She now registers defiance by giving us her repertoire louder and more often, ignoring my terrible Nelson Eddy imitation completely. Still, I'm on her side, I think; not because I'm a musical comedy or cat lover—I'm a cat envier. They come and go through Egnep without regard for rights or borders, bound to nothing and nobody. Day or night, over roofs, up trees, through fences, under sheds; stalking birds, mice, grasshoppers, stray frogs; confronting foxes, intimidating garden-bound dogs; and still managing to spend most of the day asleep. They're the real soul of Egnep.

It's nothing without its mysteries, that's the point. Penge is your place for answers: Egnep poses eternal questions . . . For example, over the gardens, across the way, there's a window that stays wide open, summer, winter, rain, snow or fog; and from it shines a light that never goes out, dawn till dawn—I've taken sightings at the deadest hours, but the window remains open, the light still glows, a deep red. And before you leap to improper conclusions, remember this is a rear window, a pointless place to advertise. Clients of disorderly houses don't clamber over garden fences and plough across soggy flower-beds; they park their cars and ring front doorbells discreetly, like the thorough gentlemen they are. So what's going on through that open window, under that glowing red lamp, the Egnep beacon? Suburban magic, a non-stop rolling seance? Bat-keeping, moth-fancying, alternative technology? Or simply the bedroom of a short-sighted, spartan insomniac . . ? The lady of the house clips her privet by night in pyjamas, green wellies and a man's dressing gown, but this could be a coincidence.

I tell you, I've lost good money betting on the back windows of the house opposite. They have a system of rotating bedrooms that would be incredible in a farce. One month the first floor left is occupied by a small boy, the first floor right by a large man, and the ground floor left by a fat girl; next month the boy changes places with the man and the girl disappears, to be replaced by an even fatter woman; but the following month the fat girl re-appears up right, the boy moves down left and it's the man's turn to disappear—only to re-appear next month up left, displacing the fatter than fat woman, who displaces the boy who, of course, disappears. This game of musical beds is complicated by the occasional appearance of a small man who shares with the fat girl—and a large white dog who shares with everyone at random. I tried to run a book on the place, but the odds were impossible to calculate; I ended up owing my wife ten pounds.

Now. Is this family under doctor's orders—some elaborate quarantine? A fertility rite? Or is it a security precaution—spies, terrorists, supergrasses, mobsters—in *Penge* . . ? Maybe they're just neurotically democratic —or pathologically indecisive. It can't be spontaneous, I know that; there's got to be a roster pinned up somewhere. Perhaps they're nomads or travelling people who can't kick the old habits. Egnep is full of refugees from the rigid conventions of Penge—that's what it's for, after all. When it finally disappears—believe me—Penge won't have room for the casualties. Viva Egnep, then. *Floreat in æternum.*

4 *Chubb's*

Penge is a white elephants' graveyard. England is full of them, I know, but I bet our white elephants are bigger than yours. The Crystal Palace Exhibition, that must've been the first pale mammoth to peg out here—the Prince Consort's pride—and architectural skeletons have been piling up ever since. But no bone is ever left unturned. The athletics stadium stands amongst the ashes of Prince Albert's pet jumbo; a local canal has been turned into a railway, a health spa into a duckpond, a skating rink into a post office, and the post office into a branch of the Woolwich. The latest pachyderm to bite the dust is—well, let's call it Chubb's.

Chubb's was a department store, and nearly as old as the Crystal Palace itself. Built to service city commuters, white elephantiasis must've set in very early, long before the Palace burned down in '36; only Chubb's took another half century to breathe its last. We knew we had a terminal case on our hands when its flag-pole was dismantled—a public hazard, they said. It sat on top of a Wembley-type dome over the main entrance for a hundred and ten years, flying the company flag, or the Union Jack on state occasions. Without it the dome looked incomplete, castrated, to be frank. No self-respecting retail business can survive that kind of innuendo.

Man and boy, I patronised Chubb's twenty-five years, and I never began to understand how it remained solvent. Chubb's was a kind of economic Indian rope trick. It was visibly over-staffed, for a start. There were a dozen departments on three floors plus basement; walk into any of those departments any time or day of the week and there'd be two assistants standing round doing nothing in particular—dusting off the merchandise, straightening their ties and flicking ballpoint pens to prove they were alive and literate. My friend Reg says it just went to show how low the wages were and how high the profits. The goods *were* over-priced, sub-standard and obsolete, granted, but the stock hardly shifted from one year's end to the next; in fact, the store seemed deliberately arranged to deter the casual or carefree purchaser. A spending spree at Chubb's was as unthinkable as a plunging neckline at a Baptist convention.

The two deep-bosomed ladies in lingerie, for instance, guarded their curtained alcove on the ground floor like matrons in a maternity hospital. For some unknown reason, this enchanted cloister could only be reached by passing through household sundries and gardenware. Maybe symbolism was intended: Eden—forbidden fruit and all that. More likely, it was a test of the customer's nerve. No male would dare to approach within twenty yards of that bower of pink, white and black elastic, leaving a wide swathe of no man's land, across which ladies of a certain age in urgent need of support occasionally made their way, disappearing behind the headless grey torso in a pink roll-on that sat at the end of the counter—like something off a gibbet. The mystique has gone out of the foundation trade now. The *foundations* have gone out of the foundation trade. I was in a Croydon boutique the other day when a semi-nude customer stepped out of the changing room and asked me to fasten her up at the back.

The window-dressers at Chubb's could've deterred a

mob of drink-crazed looters on Cup-Final night. Crystal Palace 5—Tottenham 0. Their displays were mutton dressed up as mutton: gaggles of beige, constipated dummies, stiff with agony, got up like Doris Day without the teeth; tableaux of gimcrack dated furniture, laid out like army bed-spaces. If the windows didn't warn you off, the sales staff were absolutely guaranteed to damp your enthusiasm—not a spiel or gimmick to share between them. Probably a hang-over from Edwardian times, when shop assistants were expected to behave like housemaids and bootboys. The girl in perfumery made some effort to come to terms with post-war England, I suppose, but the effort showed—like a weight-lifter's hernia. Decimated eyebrows, black and blue lids, a surgical gash for a mouth, and a tinned peaches and frozen cream complexion. All day she stood there, arranging and re-arranging little bottles and boxes, fiddling with her ear-rings and bravely presenting her least damaged profile to the public, all six of them. Chubb's was never full; customers dribbled through, a constant slow leak from the surrounding pavements. The store advertised an annual sale, but that was surely bluff. I never met anyone who went, let alone boasted of a bargain.

Making a purchase at Chubb's was a very deliberate business, something like buying a pig in West Donegal. Choice was not a problem of course, since the range in most departments was not so much narrow as microscopic—now and then the stationery counter disappeared altogether. But once you made your choice, you had to attract the attention of a sales assistant, and these tended to become fazed by their own inactivity. There were two varieties—very old or very young. I imagine the mature and able-bodied went over the wall to Debenham's or Army and Navy. But fledglings or dotards, Chubb's soon had them house-trained. They made up the bills as if they were tablets of stone. Carbons were handled like masonic vestments. Mid-way through, there was a statutory pause, while the assistant began a by now superfluous sales pitch: 'Lovely bit of stuff this, sir.' Then came the hey-presto bit, my favourite. The bill was stuffed into a metal cylinder and poked up the pneumatic pipe, whence it vanished with a long sigh to accounts at the top of the building. Kssh . . . Whatever they did with it up there took ages, which was just as well, because in the interval the assistant slowly wrapped up your purchase in string and brown paper, with a great deal of mime and flourish and a smug 'Sunday' look—as though Chubb's were giving away gift parcels out of the goodness of their hearts. I never saw anything like it, apart, perhaps, from classical Chinese dancing.

If I've given you the impression that Chubb's was dull and uninviting, then I've misled you. Penge isn't the same without it; a great loss. Not to Reg, of course; he never lays out a penny in the retail line unless it's Co-op—that's the trouble with political idealists, they're blinded by economic theory. The attractions of Chubb's were nothing to do with commerce as such. It was a living, working parody of a department store. If comedy is the gap between expectations and performance, then it was one of the best jokes in England, a film set waiting for Jacques Tati to start shooting. Not only that—or because of that—it was a highly moral establishment. No one could pass through Chubb's without being reminded how foolish, fallible and mortal our best efforts are. A sermon of a shop—it fortified the spirit and mortified the body. I know what I'm talking about; I bought a flannel blazer from them one year. We were never meant for each other: the thing had a life and shape of its own, and after a few weeks I donated it to the Cubs for their bonfire night. It looked all wrong on the guy, too; and it wouldn't burn, either.

But the pleasures of Chubb's were practical as well as philosophical. The shop stood at a cross-roads to which it gave a name—Chubb's Corner, a junction for three bus routes. The west wing of the store was mainly used as a bus-shelter, therefore. Somewhere in the basement they had the fiercest central heating system north of Krakatoa; on a cold winter's day you could walk in at the west door, do a steady Duke of Edinburgh round the ground floor, catch the latest news in the television department and nip out the east door, thoroughly defrosted. Half the local comprehensive used to trail through at least once a day, and a lazy crocodile of senior citizens—soaking up the buckshee warmth, which made the staff so torpid the place was a shop-lifters' paradise—if there had been anything portable that was worth stealing.

Chubb's was a sort of weather-proof village green, really; a great place for meeting people you hadn't met for months and stocking up with local scandal. The further the place recedes into memory the less and less shop-like it seems, if that were possible. As an emporium it was so implausible I often wondered whether it might not be a front for some illegal organisation: a sleazy casino above accounts; drug peddling behind the shoe department; espionage in the basement; a secret entrance at the back of lingerie—Louie sent me. Reg—as usual—had a more obvious explanation: one side of the premises was leased to the Electricity Board at an exorbitant rent—another clapped-out capitalist milking the state and the poor bloody consumer, he said—simple as that. I tried to put *my* case—Chubb's as an involuntary welfare centre—but he wouldn't have it. Community welfare was a right, not an incidental privilege, he said, and planning was more cost-effective. You can't argue with that logically. Except, nothing is ever as logical as it seems. A world without geriatric white elephants would be too cocksure for comfort. Take away incompetence and vulgarity and what's left? Not a lot to laugh about, really.

Chubb's basement said it all. There was a restaurant down there, Odeon style in verdigris and cream, and a long, low room with a queasy green carpet that called itself a banqueting suite. They sold the worst coffee down there I've ever tasted—barring the time my daughters mistook gravy powder for instant; and they put on a lunch whose three courses were exactly that: three courses—in endurance, initiative and resourcefulness. A plaque outside the banqueting suite announced that the Rotarians met there once a month for lunch. Inexplicable this—I mean, your business man is supposed to be a connoisseur of flesh-pots. The ones I meet are on to the subject of victuals and vintage before you can say 'Mouton Rothschild'. Which is how Chubb's hooked them, of course; the menus were always handwritten in French—incorrect French, bound in red leather with gilt edges; and the china and tableware were first-class. Someone knew their sociological onions in that catering department. Reg says the English vice is not child-beating, buggery or strikes but bogus gentility.

I'm amazed Reg was ever agin Chubb's; it confirmed his prejudices so completely—and never more so than at Christmas. Reg loathes the festive season with a fierce, fixed loathing that grows fiercer and more fixed as the shopping days lurch by; he's a committed Scrooge the three ghosts would have no chance frightening, never mind converting. Christmas is the Emperor's New Clothes, he says, with all the grown-ups playing

Emperor and all the kids taking hush money . . . Christmas at Chubb's began in October. A medium-size, illuminated Christmas tree appeared above the East door and three small dittos above the West. Under the Wembley-type dome hung a cardboard sign: 'Come and see Father Xmas, in his moon rocket/fairy grotto/giant's castle/Disney dingle/magic fall-out shelter'—depending on the year and the fancy of the manager. Father Xmas himself was a regular booking, a rosy-cheeked and very taciturn local alcoholic. He wore his white viscose cotton whiskers with a resigned, troubled air, as though he suspected the experience wasn't real but an annual attack of the jim-jams. It was no way to treat a ten pints a night man, certainly. He'd sit at the back of the over-heated, under-stocked toy department, sweltering inside his moon rocket or whatever, and go a whole hour without interviewing a single tiny client, not one of whom did he ever get to sit on his knee. In fact, I know one little girl who bit him when he insisted; her parents had to take him to Lewisham Hospital for an anti-tetanus, his beard twisted round the back of his neck like a pony-tail. From then on he always kept a good yard between him and visiting infants.

On the whole he was more sinned against than sinning, but his best friend couldn't have claimed he was a boost to the Santa Claus industry. My elder daughter paid him a single memorable visit, at the advanced age of three. Next night we just happened to mention that FC would be making the traditional call at her bedside on Christmas Eve. Well, of course, being a sensible, nicely brought-up girl, she refused to go anywhere near her bed after that; screamed loud enough to bring the social workers in. The thought of this Chubb's character—or any other old codger in a tatty red dressing-gown—the thought of *him* blundering round her room in the dark scared her witless, and quite rightly. In the end we had to expose the whole Teutonic works for the parental fraud it was; I never felt so sheepish in all my life. Other people seem to get away with murder. A friend of mine used to dress up in the full white whiskers and tatty red dressing-gown, year after year, an annual bedtime cabaret, complete with original dialogue. 'Whoa there! Stay downstairs, reindeer!' His son must've been half daft—or insufferably condescending.

Frustrated by the poor audience response to his seasonal offerings, Chubb's manager sometimes drove the resident tatty red dressing-gown out on the pavement, to bark for business. He'd shuffle up and down in front of the windows, mumbling through his beard at the constipated shop-dummies: 'Come and see my great big red rocket (or whatever).' Pedestrians crossed to the other side of the road, and lorry drivers made the obvious remarks, as only lorry drivers know how. Chubb's manager knew not what he managed; a white elephant's mahout should've known better. His shop was an institution apart, like the constitutional monarchy, say. Buying and selling at Chubb's Corner was the same as ruling and governing at Buck House—a charming fiction, that's all.

Quite honestly, I don't think the loss of our very own chain store has caused that much inconvenience, always excluding the haberdashery counter. But then, the disappearance of haberdashery counters amounts to a national emergency, something on a par with acid rain or Dutch elm disease. There was a time, whenever two or three shops were gathered together in the name of Mammon, you'd find a haberdasher's, equipped with one of those Aladdin's cave show-cases—all little drawers, troughs and trays, overflowing with buttons, ribbons, tape and zips—everything in the ancient pedlar's repertoire, and everything priced in pence. Not that I went in for these knick-knacks much myself, but the knowledge that anything you needed in the way of an appendage was *there*, ready to hand, very reassuring that. However, what I meant to say was, Pengeians mourn Chubb's not like an old-established business gone bust, but like a deceased eccentric aunt, who knitted you unwearable presents of socks and cardigans, and remembered shaking hands with George Formby. Life isn't the same, life isn't quite life, without her.

Deceased eccentric aunts aren't usually cut up and sold in second-hand chunks, but that was to be Chubb's fate. Accounts and ladies' modes are now vacant office space; lingerie and the Father Xmas habitat have metamorphosed into the Regency Billiard and Snooker Club—a wet-look plastic sun-blind ogles pot-blackers, like a pair of false eyelashes. The old banqueting suite has also sprouted wet-look shades and is now the Regency Banqueting Suite, with a non-stop calendar of dinner-dances. The west wing is boarded up, the east wing empty, the space between occupied by a good-as-new and a plumbers' merchant. Reg says it should have been turned into a community centre, the whole shebang. Maybe, in a well-ordered world; but in a well-ordered world eccentric aunts would be fairy godmothers and do amazing things with pumpkins. The truth is, Chubb's Corner is now all corner and no Chubb's, a fare-stage on a bus-route, no longer a destination; a sign of the times. Penge itself is only a bend on the London-Croydon road, these days, a kind of metropolitan elbow or funny bone—funny peculiar, that is, funny painful, even; and more so now that Chubb's is gone. Perhaps white elephants should be a protected species.

5 *Kith*

To hear my friend Reg talk, you'd think Penge was a cross between Las Vegas and Stalag Luft Three. 'The greedy fingers of the Stock Exchange are throttling the life out of this society,' he says. 'My kids are growing up in a consumer jungle. Dog eat dog,' he says. In actual fact, Reg's children are more or less grown up already; and dog *lick* dog would be nearer the mark, teenagers in Penge stick to each other like egg stains on an old pullover. Little Reg—Reg's son—is still going around with the same dubious bunch of characters he met on his first day at nursery school. This is an association of sixteen years I'm talking about, sixteen years' hard, a juvenile within the meaning of the Act, occupying a legal position somewhere between a lunatic and an off-season grouse. As a survival course it beats anything the SAS put on.

I tell you, when you've muffed your entrance in the school nativity play together, got left behind on a day-trip to Boulogne together, faked your biology field work together, kissed Justine Barker, dyed your hair, failed Geography 'A' level and sign on at the same social security office together—then you've got solidarity, the way the Matterhorn has rocks: right down the middle. There have been additions and subtractions over the years, of course, but the inner core of that group is bonded closer than the confessional, harder than the Bar Association, stronger than the nuclear force; compared to them, the Politburo or the Mafia are still wearing Lplates. Old Reg tends to be dismissive about his offspring and their peers. 'I've seen the future,' he says, 'and it won't work. They're unpolitical, unmotivated,' he says. Well I, for one, give thanks for it. If that lot ever set their minds to the business of government, it will be a case of today Penge, tomorrow . . . Well, the Elephant and Castle, at least.

As an ex-baby-sitter, unemployed teacher and feckless father, I've no illusions whatever about the latent powers of the young. I remember taking Little Reg and Little More (Big Maureen is Reg's wife)—the kids must've been about five or six at the time—I remember taking them to a park where they played with some friends: a game of tag, or it looked like a game. Last summer, marooned in the sandpit with my own apprentice teeny-boppers, I noticed the same old gang playing the same old tag—*fourteen* years on. I thought I'd flipped for a minute. Fourteen years . . . Voices had deepened, chests expanded, hair sprouted, but recognisably the same determined, deceptively innocent faces. If this be fun, I thought, there is method in it.

When you monitor Little Reg or Little More's conversation, you pick up references to quite a number of these strange rituals. Black Hole, for instance. This illegal act takes place at midnight on a local putting green. It requires a hockey stick, a billiard ball and a pair of luminous Doc Martin boots; otherwise the rules are the same as for clock golf, although a look-out is a useful option. A squad car crept up on the celebrants one night. Prepared for vandalism, orgies or worse, the constables were overcome by culture shock and joined in the game.

Until they all graduated from pedal power, the teen scene included a kind of cycle-delic rally, in a car-park, somewhere east of Pratts Bottom. The point and form of this wasn't altogether clear, but there has to be a compelling reason to go to Pratts Bottom at any time. More confidential yet is the Feast of the Magic Mushroom. This delicacy is harvested from a certain municipal recreation ground every October—Little Reg came home from football practice high as a kite last autumn, and sang all the shower-room songs in front of the Wombles—including several verses I've never heard before. Still, this sacred fungus stuff worried me, so I tackled the park superintendent. 'It's Nature,' he said, 'nothing we can do. Short of cementing over the water garden. And it won a GLC prize this year. Be thankful they're not sniffing glue,' he said. 'That's in season all year round.' He had a point, I suppose.

From what I gather, most of these ceremonials are unisex; I envy them that. In my salad days the sexes were separated by an invisible Maginot line—that is, we could've walked round it if we'd had the nous. Little Reg and his buddies seem to have *some* men-only perks, the South London, lower-middle-class, cadet equivalent of Boodles or the Beefsteak: the Penge Petomaniacs (spot the 'A' Level French candidates). There is only one club rule apparently: each member has to make regular contributions to an archive tape recording of the membership breaking wind—I'm told they have two hours' worth in the can at the moment, both solo and orchestrated pieces. Little Reg calls it a major work of (f)art (at bottom he is his father's son, I'm afraid).

The Petomaniacs are also addicted to board games, the way some people are addicted to poker; all-night sessions are quite common. They've even invented their *own* board game. It's based on the family life of one of the members. His father has been married three times, three and two half times, to be exact. The game has penalty points like tea with step-mother, new baby, social-worker, and so on; bonus points include decree nisi, holiday with granny, and lovers' tiff. They call it 'Alimony' and had plans to market their product, but then they remembered dad in question was a solicitor. Children can be surprisingly vague about what their progenitors get up to during the day: nights and weekends are another matter.

The distaff side has its exclusive rites, too—much less frivolous, naturally. Little More and friends seem to run a twenty-four hour counselling service for each other. Reg's phone bills are enormous; he threatened to put a lock on the dial. 'I see,' said Little More, 'Czechoslovakia. All over again.' And Red Reg crumbled. Kitchen encounter groups push up his beverage bill, too. 'Dialectic and coffee go together,' says Little More cunningly. And Big More buys in another jar of instant effluent. 'Keeps them off the streets,' she says. A joke, though I'm not so sure. These first-born feminists were weaned on solid protest; they've been to more demonstrations than I've had dental fillings. Causes at some remove from good old Reg's vintage class struggle: Women's Rights, Abortion, Third World Development, Scrap Cruise. Reg tells them, they can't see the wood for the trees. And Little More tells *him*, you can't see the wood till you're out of it.

But they're not just lemon-sharp and street-wise, these *jeunes filles*, they join hands with Auntie Jane Austen as well. I know of no other social group so dedicated to the dying art of English letter writing. They're at it continually, penning notes in the morning to friends they're about to meet the same afternoon; scribbling long notes to friends they only left half-an-hour ago; curt, anonymous notes to enemies they never want to meet again; receiving reams from friends who've been away; sending regular volumes to friends who are never coming back. Sad notes, serious notes, silly notes, smutty notes, threatening notes, coded notes, pleading notes, needling notes; bursting into red, green, black, brown, blue long-hand, when and wherever they come to rest; indoors, outdoors, on buses, trains, the backs of motorbikes, and once in mid-air—three thousand feet up—on a charity parachute jump. (Little More swears to it, honest.) All vividly illustrated or decorated, like mediæval manuscripts. It's compulsive; Saint Paul and Lord Chesterfield aren't in it.

When Little More baby-sat for us, she used to leave little coloured notes all round the house—we're still running into them years afterwards. 'Can't find disposable nappies. Used this tank-top . . . Hope you're having a good evening, because I'm not . . . Thank God for the pill, I'll never be a mother.' This was illustrated by a drawing of a fat, smug ovum carrying a placard, SPERMS GO HOME. For some unknown reason, teachers are always intercepting and destroying these nuggets, when they should be actively encouraging a remarkable new art form. Fortunately these compulsive correspondents are compulsive hoarders. Little More has an old shoe-box stuffed full of the things—material of a PhD in years to come, mark my words: Aspects of Social Literacy and Gender Reinforcement amongst Female Adolescents in Late Twentieth-Century Conurbations. The fat, smug ovum will have a whole paragraph to herself.

Now you mustn't get the idea that the Youth of Penge are unusual in any way. No. They go in for all the normal amusements, from church youth clubs to beer and space invaders, from the Young Trots to video-nasties and the Young Conservatives. But these facilities are dished-up by their elders and betters; their own life is elsewhere, safely tucked away so the elders can't find it. Sympathetic, understanding parents create problems, therefore.

I remember when Little Reg and Little More started to stay out late at parties. Big R and Big M went at it like a couple of eager curates: cosy chats about responsibility and hormones, and would Little More like to speak to nice Dr Sexton. The juniors were cool, distinctly huffy—not to say disgusted—by this one-dimensional attitude to what they did in the small hours. Little More came up to our place for a quiet weep.

'My parents are really seamy,' she said. 'You'd think they'd notice I was a *person*, not just an appetite on legs.'

I tried to explain. How different it was in Mummy-and-Daddy-o's day. Being young was considered an aberration then, sex was pronounced with an asterisk, supposing you dared to use the word, and mixed company carried an X-certificate.

'Poor them,' said Little More. 'Why don't *they* go and speak to nice Dr Sexton?'

These parties Little Reg and his sister attend are not quite the excuse for loose goings-on that their father imagines. I don't say they're religious retreats exactly, but, unlike the parties in my day, they have no single ulterior motive—lust, I mean. They celebrate a whole range of pleasures: artistic, aesthetic, sensual, communal, musical, intellectual. The one-track dirty mind has been replaced by the multi-track disposable life-style. Parties are custom-built now, *designed*, like movies—inspired by movies, sometimes. Monty Python parties, Superman parties, Casablanca parties; 'Fifties' parties, 'Sixties' parties, Arab parties, Russian parties; Clown parties, Action Man parties, Fruit-and-Veg parties (Little More went as a banana and split her skin); Actress and Bishop parties, Sackcloth and Ashes parties, Anti-Trouser parties, Anti-Party parties—*scores* of parties, every week-end, from Beckenham to Bermondsey, a circuit as real and tangible as the South Circular Road, and almost as crowded.

I've known young Pengeians hop from one to another, up to four in a night. Gate-crashing—if accompanied by a sponsor—seems to be the done thing. This produces some wonderful cheek-by-jowling. South London has always been a heady social and ethnic mix, but now . . . Daughters of junior government ministers in Greenwich dance with sons of petty criminals from Penge; sons of National Theatre directors in Blackheath pour real ale for daughters of school care-takers from Lewisham; the son of a millionaire socialist builder argues with the nephew of an impoverished Tory poet.

Accents give the mix a final stir—down South the *lingua franca* of the comprehensive school is spoken by the sons of lawyers and labourers alike. One of Little Reg's pals was taken up by the daughter of a trendy novelist from Dulwich. Randy for the arms of a genuine man of the people, she dropped him like a skip of hard-core once she met his parents. Schoolteachers with impeccable, laboriously acquired received pronunciation. 'We've read all your father's books, dear. Absolutely marvellous. Another *petit-four*. . . ?' End of relationship.

I've been involved in two of those parties myself. There was the Breakfast party at Reg's place. Platoons of pyjama-clad adolescents invaded his kitchen at seven-thirty one morning, brandishing spoons and cereal bowls—no alcohol. They got stinking drunk on corn-flakes and muesli. Honest. The old forget, when you're young you can get drunk on anything, or nothing at all. Reg is still recovering from the shock of all that raw energy. 'We must harness it,' he keeps saying, as if his kids were Morecambe Bay or the Severn Bore. Which they are, of course. *I'm* still recovering from the Pimps and Tarts party. Intrigued by the thoroughness of Little

More's preparations, I was fool enough to ask her to drop by *en route*, and show us the results.

We arrived home one evening to find a dozen rouged and fish-netted ladies of the street standing on the front lawn, in a variety of provocative and very convincing poses. Knowing me to be unemployed, some of my neighbours have since put two and two together and made one. As matter of fact, I seem to have displaced the glamorous widow down the road as the local *succès de scandale*. But it wasn't just the whores' parade that did it; *that* was only a beginning.

Later the same night, or rather early next morning, some pseudo pimps and tarts are walking back from the party when one of the girls passes out on the pavement—the legendary newt. However, since they're close by our place, Little More comes round to ask if I'll ferry the casualty home. And suddenly there I am, dead of night, *in flagrante*, shovelling a prostrate young tart into the back of our Mini-traveller, with the assistance of a second (tipsy) tart, and a couple of boozy pimps—slouch hats, dark glasses, two-tone shoes, the full rig—all three of them giggling away like blocked sinks. And there was worse to come.

When we reach the casualty's home—she's more or less conscious now—she discovers her key is missing, and begs me to effect an illegal entry through a rear window. It appears she's terrified of her father, a psychiatrist. You'd think a psychiatrist would have better things to do than put the fear of God into his own daughter, but still . . . We trek round the house—me, the two tarts, and the boozy pimps, whose giggles are becoming hysterical. I aim a kick at them and bang my knee on a wheelbarrow; and wish it had been a brick wall, because the pimps immediately grab it and start giving each other rides; round and round the rockery, shrieking and laughing, over the moon. By this time it's too late to go back, so I blunder on, like King Kong on the Empire State building.

I'm hoisting the shrink's comatose daughter up through a convenient fan-light—half-garotted by her wiry, fish-net thighs, well-nigh choking on her ra-ra skirt—when down the garden path pads papa shrink himself, waving a flashlight and what looks like an old baseball bat. Of course, Little More and the pimps turn and do an instant bunk, don't they? And the terrified daughter disappears with a scream and a convulsive wriggle into the interior, leaving me clutching an empty ra-ra skirt. I'd have disappeared too, but my bruised knee had gone stiff. 'Just seeing the little lass home,' I said, offering up the skirt.

Papa shrink didn't say anything, so I hung the skirt on his baseball bat and backed away, tripping over the abandoned wheelbarrow. He just stood there shaking. It was two o'clock in the morning and he was only wearing pyjamas, but I thought trick-cyclists were meant to be unshakeable—we'd obviously made an impression. 'Don't be too hard on her,' I suggested, as I hobbled out the gate. 'We're only young once.' An old baseball bat whistled past my ear and buried itself deep in the garden hedge. What Freud would've made of it all, I don't know . . . Incidentally, the poor feller subsequently made enquiries about this mysterious, lame, skirt fetishist in his garden, but Little More never let on. The trick-cyclist's daughter didn't appear at a party for another year, though.

This wasn't the punishment her father intended, however; by no means. Because, you see, the most important social event amongst young Pengeians today is not the Party but the Gathering. The Gathering. A gathering is simply an informal but regular meeting of friends; it may be planned or spontaneous, be held by day or by night, for two or twenty people, for one or twenty hours. It may involve music, eating and drinking; equally, it may not. Above all, its proceedings are deadly secret, impenetrable. Ask Young Penge about its parties and they'll tell you, if they're in the mood and you ask nicely—they are their own favourite topic of conversation, after all. But gatherings are something else.

Secrecy is maintained by a curious practice: circular—or endogamous—dating. It works something like this. Little Reg goes out with Joanna, who previously went out with Jonathan, who has started going steady with Sarah, who up until now went steady with Little Reg—since he stopped going around with Erica, that is, who now goes around with Craig, who previously saw a lot of Joanna, who'd previously been attached to Jonathan. When you know that Jonathan also saw a lot of Craig at one time, and they'd been close to Vanessa before she went away to college with Jim, who still writes every week to Erica, you'll begin to see what I'm driving at.

Last month two of Little Reg's mob interrupted their honeymoon to attend a gathering. This summer one of these clans went off busking in Barcelona. Couldn't play, scarcely sing, but they came back festooned with pesetas and photographs of ripe Catalan beauties—of both sexes. Another clan went grape-picking round Bordeaux—a glass of Tesco's medium-white will never taste the same again. What we're seeing in action here is—the future, I *think*. Maybe it won't work, as Reg says, but it's busy enough. I get tired just looking at it.

6 *Common Ground*

Civil war has come to Penge—very discreetly, as you'd expect; to be honest, imperceptibly. But it's happening, here in the forgotten southland, beyond the Metropolitan and Victoria Lines. As an unwaged house-husband and Pengeologist, I watch dog owners and joggers go out to do battle daily. The fleet of foot and the four of foot are up in arms, so to speak—or more accurately, the flat of foot and the six of foot. Out on the streets, for the sake of appearances, an uneasy truce is maintained; in the wilder regions of the public parks and recreation grounds, take it from me, guerrilla warfare rages. The bye-laws ought to give joggers the edge there, of course, but ancient custom works in favour of the doggers. Four generations of blind eyes, turned to the NO DOGS EXCEPT ON LEAD signboard. That amounts to—well, squatters' rights. I choose my words carefully.

Penge is witnessing an epic territorial struggle—or it would be if it was looking. Cowboys and Indians across the council prairies; high-noon down the mean-minded terraces; for quiet, concentrated bloody-mindedness, the conflict takes some beating. The vandal, soccer nut, illegal cyclist or kamikaze breakdancer are familiar—almost expected—terrors of the park. Now the middle-aged barbarians are moving in. The other day I saw two elderly joggers go for a Sealyham while its owner was retrieving a rubber ball. The Sealyham hadn't a leg to stand on—legally, I mean. It had no business snapping at marathon buffs and lolloping about the football pitch: keep-fit canines have their very own paddock behind the tennis courts, specially reserved. My friend Reg calls it Excrement Gulch, although he still insists on ploughing across it five or six times a week, wet or dry. The shock absorbers on his Taiwan trainers might have been designed to scoop up the stuff, and transport it back to his living-room carpet. I suppose if I were a Sealyham I'd find that provocative—or a Doberman for that matter, not to mention Big More, Reg's wife. Reg has invented a new sport, she says: turd trekking. All you need is a pair of legs, a pair of deep-pattern soles—and the great pet-loving British public does the rest.

Reg reckons he took up jogging as a political act. Big More says their new bathroom mirror drove him out on the streets, in self-disgust. But Reg can't change his socks without getting his ideology right.

'It's the first cheap sport for the masses,' he says.

'Seems a pretty solitary activity to me,' I say.

'You've never been on a fun-run. That's a metaphor for the British road to socialism,' he tells me.

I point out that they all looked totally knackered at the end of the road.

'Inside they're glowing with fulfilment,' he explains.

'It's ninety per cent masochismo,' I insist. 'Male chauvinists chasing their own tails. Round and round.'

'Don't mention dogs; even metaphorically,' he barks . . .

It was Reg who first drew my attention to the civil war. Staggering home up the avenue one dark night, a local mutt took a fancy to his loaded soles, tripped him up, tore a lump out of his tracksuit. He took refuge at our place, repressed bourgeois indignation bursting out of him like a punctured hose pipe.

'I pay rates, I pay taxes—four or five grand per

annum. But for 37p that bung-nosed, four-legged fascist thug can pollute and terrorise the whole neighbourhood —37p, a licence to spread fear and smear . . .'

You'd have thought, with rising 20 per cent unemployment, exponential economic decline, and the nation run by a cast of third-rate amateurs reading a duff script, that a member of the Lewisham Radical Front might have more important things to complain about. However, as a floating—or rather drowning—voter, with two ageing cats who make our side-entry look like the Cloaca Maxima on a Bread and Circus day, I am in no position to criticise. Moreover, my scrappy classical education was acquired on the rates.

Reg's indignation is understandable; late converts to jogging have a lot to contend with. They trot out morning or evening, keeping themselves to themselves, harmless primitives, health and happiness their only aim. And sedentary neighbours respond by twitching curtains derisively, or leering behind their backs. Joggers receive so many pitying, you'll-regret-it glances, they feel obliged to simulate constant, strenuous pleasure. The unnecessary strain causes most of their injuries, I'm sure. Along the streets clumps of pubescent girls mock their progress, jeering lewdly and shrieking: 'Hup-one-two, hup-one-two!' Pubescent girls in Penge seem to find all masculine physical activity suggestive. Little boys, on the other hand, take it far too seriously. They embarrass menopausal joggers by trotting beside them and—more often than not—overtaking them, shaming them into a pretence that they're winding down after a ten-mile circuit: much glancing at watch, wiping of brow, dangling of wrists and so forth.

A hundred yards of this pantomime and they're completely exhausted, of course. They slow to a grateful halt, only to discover some colleague or acquaintance appearing round the next corner but one, which necessitates a sudden confident burst of speed, to impress the onlooker. Before they can decently catch their breath, this catapults them into the High Street at the height of the rush hour, exposing them to the cold scrutiny of returning commuters. Nine times out of ten a desperate lunge for the nearest side street—and the chance of a dignified collapse against a garden wall—runs them slap into a sun-tanned, startlingly young fellow jogger, who surges past with a superior smile. A defiant reckless sprint leaves our hero—or heroine—with spots before the eyes, ringing in the ears, burning in the chest, and knees with two minds of their own. To be confronted at this point by an unsympathetic dog eager to inspect your ankles, buttocks or pelvis must be the final humiliation.

On the face of it, a trot round the park seems to offer comparative peace and quiet: nothing to cope with but hyperactive kids and sceptical park keepers. Council park-keepers are trained never to move at more than two miles an hour, until whistle-blowing time or a national emergency, whichever comes sooner. Have you ever seen a park keeper *run*? However, jogging hours, unfortunately, tend to clash with prime dog-walking periods, or rather dog-releasing—something to do with bio-rhythms, I expect. Three or four times a day flats, maisonettes and semis disgorge a bewildering regiment of breeds, mixed-breeds, muddle-breeds and mutants, bounding into every corner of the park, and marking it for their very own; while their doting licensees notch up the decibels like company sergeant-majors, bawling across the flower beds in a kitsch doggy dialect made up entirely of names—Scamp, Spot, Rajah, Rameses, Sinbad and Chu-Chu. I've noticed that the largest dogs with the grandest titles generally come from newer, smaller houses, and the smallest animals with cosy, twee names from great barns of Victorian villas.

Whatever their background, dogs rarely take any notice of the drill-sergeants' chorus. If they did, I'd suggest the answer to the dogger-jogger conflict would be to license the runners, and provide them with minders, too. It seems most unfair that they not only have to fend off the beasts but engage in verbal abuse with their owners at the same time. As it is, I don't think an armistice is possible without major advances in modern medicine; both dogging and jogging are addictive, you see. It will take new drugs to bring an end to this war. I tell you, a nervous friend of Reg's never sets off on a jog without a lump of stewing steak as a peace offering—he got the idea from a cat-burglar when he was on jury service. Reg himself has been known to go out wearing leather gauntlets, with a short lasso and a small shillelagh, inscribed A GIFT FROM CONNEMARA, stuffed up his vest. He's a pacifist and it's the only weapon he possesses. What they'd say at Bromley hospital if he was knocked over by a bus, I can't imagine.

Frankly, Reg hasn't been the same since the night he passed out jogging through the subway at New Beckenham station. He was labouring up into the lamplight when he heard the pad of large paws, pounding and echoing in the dim tunnel behind him. Turning, bleary-eyed from fatigue, he beheld a shaggy, four-foot-high hound with flashing white teeth, thundering down upon him. Astride it rode a wild-eyed dwarf in brown doublet and hose. With a yell Reg flung himself to one side, grazed his chin on a bollard and lost consciousness briefly. He struggled back home, slunk indoors and rang me. He'd jogged himself into an hallucinatory high, he said, his voice an octave higher than usual. And not to worry the wife, but which of the Health Centre doctors would I recommend?

After I'd calmed him down a bit I was able to suggest, as the unofficial recorder of Penge, that what he'd actually seen was the daughter of the local pet shop owner returning from the Brownies' hut, on the back of a Shetland pony her father was trying to flog—sell, that is. Reg has never quite believed this explanation. He now aerobes himself more carefully, runs shorter distances at a much slower pace, keeps to parks and open spaces wherever possible, and goes armed at full moon—or when he's feeling Ides of Marchish, which on average is about once a week and twice on Sundays. Foreboding is more regular than sex with our Reg.

Contemporary Penge is short on parks and open spaces it can call its own. I don't count the rambling pleasuredrome and ruins of Crystal Palace Park—the whole of London has appropriated that, and the best of rural Penge was snapped up to create it in the first place. I suspect some wily eighteenth-century squire enclosed a common or two as well. We only have a few flat acres to mooch about in now, although we're surrounded by other people's broader acres: the rolling parkland of Beckenham Place, the ornamental splendours of Dulwich and Horniman Gardens, the timeless panoramas of One Tree Hill. To be short on local parks is a great loss; they're the closest we get to village greens here in the suburbs. Places where loitering, gossip, gawping and boondoggling are allowed free expression. Elsewhere these inalienable rights quickly become criminal offences.

That's a lesson the unemployed soon learn. When I started life on the dole I often used to spend a happy hour looking out of the launderette window, just watching the world go by. The swish and gurgle of other people's dirty linen is very restful. Washing was traditionally a communal activity, you recall, and I've always thought that launderettes could easily double as salons or art centres—soap opera might take on an entirely new meaning. When I broached the subject to the *concierge* woman they have in these establishments, she wasn't keen, didn't fancy the Lilian Bayliss part at all. 'Piss off out of it,' she said. Which was fair enough, in a way, because we did all our washing at home. It's very hard simply to *be* somewhere these days; society requires you to be *doing* something all the time, or *en route* to doing it and, ideally, paying to do it.

My first six months as a househusband, I was made to feel very uncomfortable—an able-bodied younger man, wandering about Penge in broad daylight. There were only three categories of wanderer then: the retired, the retarded and the recidivist. Reg's son, Little Reg, told me, via the school grapevine, that the glamorous widow over the way had me down as a copper's nark; the single ladies next door thought I was suffering from an incurable illness (well, I am—curiosity); and the superannuated railwayman six doors down still thinks I'm a gigolo. This is hysterically funny, according to my wife—I really don't see why; after all, it says more about the railwayman's shortcomings than mine. Little Reg said it was the way I walked—body language, he explained. Shortly afterwards I slipped a disc, and was flat on my back for a month. It takes a shrewd man to retain his innocence in this world, believe me.

It seems that unemployment is more acceptable nowadays. The Major Problem of the Age is never out of the news. There's even a sort of seedy status in being one of the vital statistics, like the page three girl in *The Sun*. But the big difference is, you can lose yourself in the crowd—not that we ever form a crowd, although a lot of us gravitate to a park once or twice a day, communing if not communicating.

'You should be forming action groups to combat the evils of monetarism,' says Reg.

'Public meetings aren't allowed in the park,' I remind him.

'John Ball and the Peasants' Revolt managed all right on Blackheath,' he says.

'If you want the unemployed to listen to your rubbish,' I mumble, 'you'd better learn to speak their bloody language.'

He didn't talk to me for weeks after that, and then it was only to ask the times of the trains to Croydon.

In the park you can recognise the unemployed by the way they walk: a kind of tense, shifty saunter, very different from the aimless amble of the retired, or the lazy shuffle of the convalescent. My guess is, we're all seeking refuge in some sort of pastoral idyll, some England that never was or can be. A suburban park will always retain a hint of that, no matter how much of Disneyland they introduce. A Penge recreation ground at dusk has a touch of pathos about it, with the keeper's chains rattling, and his whistle echoing back from the bowling pavilion, and the dusty patch of nature he guards, banged up in the dark like a prisoner—the night surrendered to the street lamps, and the raucous traffic, and the endless brick and concrete. I'm surprised the keepers don't sob out loud. Of course they're well aware the park doesn't remain unoccupied during the night; the pastoral idyll still casts its spell over rowdies, revellers and randies.

Once upon a time the parks department tried to discourage them, by demolishing their favourite haunts—you must remember those wooden shelters? Shabby Victorian or Edwardian verandas smothered in graffiti, with battered cubicles and shattered benches, where old men dozed and young boys swarmed and lovers loved; where nice ladies knitted, and tired mothers rocked perambulators. The council began by boarding up the cubicles, so the local lads ripped off the roof as a reprisal. When it was fenced off and corrugated over they set fire to it. Who did what and why has never been very clear to me, but between them they razed it to the ground in the end. Nowhere left to dodge out of the rain; nowhere to mope and moon. A vague promise of a fibre-glass canopy—I ask you. It's part of the new philosophy: keep on the move, curtail arrivals, cut departures—all through-put, no stay-put. Across the park, sniff the blossom, breathe the air, out you go. I know characters who only see parks and commons as short cuts to somewhere else. Two or three years ago a late-night Penge reveller in a hurry clambered over some spiked railings, slipped, caught his jacket and choked to death, head-down above the wallflowers. The pastoral idyll is not mocked, perhaps.

I'm absolutely certain that open spaces in the suburbs invite disaster; they seem to cancel or over-ride your instinct for self-preservation. I've gone walkabout over most of South London's parks and commons, first with Reg's kids and now my own. And I recognise the dangers—without ever being able to avoid them, naturally. A few weeks back I was traversing the local rec, shambling along minding my own business, wondering how my vegetable casserole was doing, when I heard a wittering from the swing enclosure. A little girl was in distress—mind you, she deserved to be.. The place was littered with carefully designed play equipment; none of your rusty iron whirligigs that I risked life and limb on, no: gaily painted aluminium frames to clamber over, polystyrene animals to ride, plastic-coated swings to swing. But children can't abide the obvious, improvisation is what turns them on. This girl had found a metal pole supporting a noticeboard next to the attendant's shed. She'd shinned up it, and then slid down again, trapping her right leg between the pole and the shed, which was minus its attendant, of course.

I'd have left her to the park-keeper and fire brigade, only her older sister appealed to me, a slender willowy girl with wide blue eyes and honey-coloured hair. Mills and Boon beckoned.

'Don't worry,' I said. 'What she pushed in, we can pull out.' But we couldn't. She screamed blue murder. 'Don't worry,' I said, 'We can lever the pole away.'

'You must be very strong,' she breathed.

'Fairly,' I said.

That did it. Up the pole I went, over the head of the wretched girl, leaned back against the shed, inserted my foot in the gap, and pushed at the pole. After three goes, my heart pounding, my forehead damp and my cunningly concealed bald patch exposed—the beautiful sister pulled her free.

'Oh, thank you,' she murmured, in a husky voice.

'It was nothing,' I said, relaxing. Agony: my knee and ankle were firmly wedged between hut and pole; I couldn't budge. Feeling slightly sick, I clung to the pole, five feet above the ground, frantically wrenching at my leg. Something clicked.

'Are you all right?' The blue eyes smiled up at me from under the honey-coloured hair.

'Don't worry, have it out in a second . . .'

'Are you sure? We have to go into tea now.'

'Quite sure.'

They walked off and left me hanging there, twitching feebly, like a maggot on a hook.

It began to rain. I didn't like to call for help, it seemed

undignified. I had a vague hope my leg would cool and shrink, but it didn't.

'What the hell you playing at?' asked the park-keeper, forty minutes later.

'A little girl got stuck,' I moaned.

'Oh, *her*, she's always doing it. *You* ought to know better.'

He fetched a crow-bar from the shed and released me. I crashed down, scraping my nose against the pole. When I tried to stand up I fell over again; he had to send for an ambulance, and was very huffy because whistle-blowing time was delayed by ten minutes. They invoiced me ten pounds or something for the ambulance, and I'm still walking with a limp.

But that was nothing to what I endured a couple of years ago: number one daughter got me into it. Her lust for novelty and adventure seems insatiable, and she doesn't know what physical fear *is*. Two years ago she developed this passion for climbing trees and, not wishing to stunt her education or deprive her of a potentially rewarding experience, I encouraged her; more, I abetted her, bye-laws or no bye-laws. So, one hot Sunday summer afternoon, it became my pleasant duty to help her tackle a challenging beech tree, in a quiet corner of Beckenham Place Park. Fifteen fun-packed minutes later we had reached the third tier of branches, and found a comfortable perch, where we could rest before descending. It was very peaceful up there; the wood was hushed, no wind, hardly a rustle. We lay back against the trunk and peered through the leaves at the sky above—under the greenwood tree, who loves to lie with me, and all that. Unfortunately, when I looked down again, a pair of ardent young lovers had crept beneath our perch, and were dallying away with a will towards a wordless but, hopefully, satisfying conclusion.

This would have been awkward in almost any circumstances, but my daughter hadn't got too far in biology and ethics at this stage—she was six and a half—so I had an extra problem. And immediately solved it, by taking the coward's way out.

'Shh,' I whispered.

'What, Daddy?'

'Shh. They're playing a game down there, and we don't want to spoil it, do we?'

'No, Daddy. Where?'

'Don't look.'

'Why not?'

'It's rude, you know that. Just sit here quiet and I'll whisper you a story.'

We sat in the tree and I started on *Squirrel Nutkin*—a stroke of genius, I thought. The stratagem would have worked a treat if she hadn't decided she wanted to spend a penny, and couldn't wait. Assisting your six-year-old daughter to relieve herself in silence, twenty feet up the north side of a beech tree, while true love finds a way at floor level on the south, is an initiative test I recommend to any army selection board. Let the Professionals try it, if they dare.

It was another half-hour before we could safely climb down, and my daughter is still talking about it, two years later. My wife says I've done irreparable psychological damage. 'Yes,' I say, 'to *me*. I had to decide. On the spot, off the cuff. Put yourself in my position,' I plead. 'I don't climb trees,' she says coldly. Neither do I any more. And I seldom step inside park gates without feeling a slight tingle up my spine. At any moment the precarious balance of Penge life could be upset by events beyond my control, I know that. Yet I never look back . . . The call of the municipal wild.

7 Seedcorn and Chips

Number two daughter has changed schools—technically, at least. A mixed infant, she was metamorphosed to a mixed junior. That's what they were called until very recently; you can still see it on school signboards and stationery. Mixed sexes we're talking about: Victorian morality lingered in England—lingers; is there still such a thing as mixed bathing? It used to be a big thrill to read that written up at the swimming baths. That was the start of the nude encounter groups and uni-sex saunas we know and love. My friend Reg says mixed bathing was the nearest he ever got to sex-education or marriage guidance. His wife says she can believe it. The honeymoon was nearly ruined when she forgot her one-piece woolly cozzie and Timothy White's swimming cap.

Anyway, number two daughter is now a junior, although I can't see much difference myself. The same school building, the same peer group, more or less. Thirty yards across the playground the infants are mixing and being infantile—business as usual. But to daughter number two it's graduation, coming out, coming of age, the Queen's commission, ordination and I don't know what. The lessons that aren't on the timetable are the ones that schools teach best; as an unemployed schoolteacher, I know. They call it the hidden curriculum. And my daughter has learned her lessons well: life's a ladder, a higher rung is better than a lower rung, and when you climb up you *rejoice*.

'We must kick the ladder away,' argues friend Reg. I tell him, the ones at the top will be laughing. 'We must replace the ladder with an escalator,' he goes on. 'The long march through the institutions begins at school.' Reg is difficult to follow sometimes, he's still chewing over the indigestible 'sixties.

'Your daughter's being brainwashed,' he says, more simply.

'Of course,' I say, 'but at the moment she's enjoying it.'

I haven't the heart to spoil her promotion. Being a junior entitles you to privileges: playing in the big playground, where there's an embankment you can jump off or roll down, if you're not caught by the caretaker; and bushes to hide behind; and a big lavatory with a mirror; and lining up in columns when the bell rings; and assembly with hymns and difficult words; and being a gerbil or dinner monitor—there's really no end to it. Above all, the opportunity to rub shoulders with enormous ten- or eleven-year-olds, labouring under the weight of soon becoming twelve, or even thirteen. My daughter came home all of a tizzy the other week, and confessed that a big boy had kissed her. 'Whereabouts did he kiss you?' I asked, wanting to put the record straight. 'In the playground,' she said. Grown-ups will be the ruin of children, something ought to be done about us before it's too late.

Old Reg walked across this minefield in classic style. The incident deserves a prize—if I didn't know him better I'd swear he made it up.

'Please, Dad,' says his seven-year-old son one day, 'Where do I come from?'

Right, thinks Reg, this is it, the gospel according to Spock. He has asked, and I will tell him, as honestly as I can, bull by the horns. And he takes little Reg through a gentle, child's guide to reproduction: tiny seeds,

Mummy's tummy, Daddy's willy, the mysteries of the belly-button, and how it was all good, beautiful and wonderfully hygienic, considering.

'Now,' says Reg, at the finish, 'do you understand?'

'Yes, Dad,' says Little Reg, very serious. 'My friend Tony said he come from Croydon.'

In the junior school the Wendy house is folded away, the story carpet rolled up, and free activities carefully controlled. Pupils are assigned to fixed seats and tables according to character and inclination. I learn that there is a Brainy table, a Funny table, a Noisy Girls' table, a Noisy Boys' table, a Slow table, and an empty table in the corner where Christopher usually sits, because Christopher is a Very Naughty boy. I've not yet established what young Christopher does exactly—a number of natural or unnatural acts suggest themselves. But my daughter just won't talk: Christopher is naughty, full-stop.

'Was he naughty in the infants?' I ask.

'Yes, but nobody stopped him.'

'Did nobody mind?'

'I don't know.'

Poor Christopher: much is forgiven an infant; a junior is judged daily.

Of course, I'm giving you number two daughter's view of things. It's not easy to understand how information filters through her head. In her first year as an infant she came home with a story about a horrible vegetable the school was looking forward to. I assumed this was fantasy and changed the subject, but she went on about it for weeks—quite adamant, she was. The whole school was preparing to enjoy this horrible vegetable. In the end I assumed it was one of those visiting theatre groups: actors in tights and *papier mâché* costumes, affecting to be Percy Potato or Terry Turnip or some other legume. Then a circular letter arrived, cordially inviting us to the Harvest Festival—the *Harvest Festival.* There are penalties in raising your children as agnostics. I'll never forget escorting Reg's lad to an Anglican christening at which communion was celebrated. When the vicar appeared with the chalice Reg's lad stared in disbelief, then he jabbed me in the ribs. 'What they doing with the FA cup?' he said loudly.

This child disinformation service must confuse the school as much as the home, yet they actively encourage the process. It's on the timetable. Every Monday morning juniors sit down to write their News—that is, they report back to school on the family weekend, in word and picture. The best reports, whatever that means, are read out in class, and a selection of those displayed on Open Day. I've got used to the idea now, but I found it very disquieting at first—I'm surprised Mrs Whitehouse hasn't latched on to it. In my opinion the mayhem of a family weekend is not suitable material for children; besides which, there are enough natural informers, grasses, snouts or whistle-blowers in any generation, without training more. There have been Mondays when I dreaded picking the kids up from school. I mean, they must have amassed enough evidence to certify me by now, and we're a dull, monogamous, basically law-abiding family. Very boring for the kids—I have twinges of guilt about it on and off.

But they've got all kinds of interesting families in that school: one-parent families, three-parent families, gay-parent families, grandparent families. I don't suppose they're any more pleased than I am to have their little idiosyncrasies noted down and proclaimed in public. Number one daughter said a description of me was read out last Monday, and everybody laughed. She refused to tell me why, but admitted she'd drawn a picture. I shall have to wait till Open Day to get at the truth; maybe I can tear the piece out of her work folder when nobody's looking. As if I hadn't got enough worries.

Number one daughter hates me going into school, you see. 'He shows off,' she explained to my wife. Anyone who knows me would absolve me of that particular failing—not many others, granted, but showing off, yes. I think she means I ask her teachers polite, informal questions and laugh encouragingly at their jokes—or is it my turquoise polo neck and the red corduroy jacket with pickle stains on the collar? Whatever the reason, I'm only allowed in school if I promise not to speak, or smile, or make any sudden movements. I feel like a walking land mine, or a comic book monster on parole. But I'm punch drunk by now. My confidence started ebbing away at our very first interview with the head.

'Are you famous?' she asked. 'One can't tell these days.'

'Well, I'm working on it,' I smiled.

'Good,' she said doubtfully. 'It does help with fêtes, and prize-giving and getting noticed by the press.'

She's suffering from withdrawal symptoms: for a while one of her parents was a famous television entertainer. Then he packed his son off to boarding school, leaving the rest of us feeling hopelessly inadequate.

I wouldn't be surprised if Open Day frightened him off—it frightens me. This is our third coming up, and the head's speech, the choir's songs, the percussion group's riffs, and a lot of the stories and drawings pinned on the walls will be desperately familiar. If the paper dragon appears in the play again I shall personally set fire to it. It's a very fine dragon that took months to make, but there are limits to the number of plots into which it can be reasonably inserted. Last year it quite ruined the point of *Peter and the Wolf*, although the wolf's costume contributed to the fiasco: it consisted of a hearth rug, furry bedroom slippers and pasteboard fangs. The rug kept slipping round the back, revealing an inside-out Marks and Spencer sweater with a hole in it.

You accept repetition in the annual Nativity play of course; that's different, that goes with the plot—God forbid it should be otherwise; believers would claim He already had, I guess. It's not the predictability of the play I object to in this case but the type-casting. Every Christmas a clear-spoken, over-confident, aggressively intelligent child shouts the narration, with the minimum of inflection and a total absence of feeling. Everybody seems in awe of this chosen one, including his proud parents, who sit in the front row dreaming of scholarships to Dulwich College and Cambridge. And a seat in the Cabinet or a Nobel Prize to crown their old age. The Virgin Mary is invariably an insipid blonde or brunette who holds the infant Jesus like a yule log and who doesn't say much—what she does you can't hear. I've never seen a Joseph yet who didn't look mortally embarrassed—quite understandably, it's the original spare part in every sense of the word. And I've never met a Chief Shepherd who had a sense of humour—stone-faces the lot of them. Consequently, they're often the funniest turn in the show. I've rarely known 'Look, the star' not to raise a smile.

On the other hand, one of the Three Kings is bound to be the school wit; the slow procession round the stage provides wonderful opportunities for a talented comedian. The black, yellow or brown boy playing middle king always knows he is making a stand for multi-ethnic education, and looks as if he'd rather do it by playing football. Angel Gabriel is often a consolation prize for the runner-up to the loud, well-spoken child, but they both prove to be equally objectionable. The cherubim and seraphim are a collection of paper and dinner monitors, with one or two difficult girls thrown in because it might be good for them. These pout and sigh and waggle their hips and look up at the ceiling, since their parents aren't there and wouldn't be seen dead on such an occasion. At the finale they surprise you by belting out 'Hark, the Herald' as though they were on the terraces at Millwall—it's the only time the production really comes to life.

Please don't think I'm blaming the teaching staff; at least half of them aren't Christian, and they're only doing what's expected, even if it doesn't come up to expectations. Reg saw that play eight times while his children were infants and juniors. His daughter, Little More, was a seraphim once, and Little Reg an apprentice shepherd. As a devout worshipper of Tony Benn, Reg wanted them to withdraw their labour, but they were eager to maintain solidarity with their peers, a good percentage of whom were Moslem, Sikh or Hindu. No wonder the Vicar of Bray is a national folk hero. When I think about it, I don't know whether to laugh or cry.

This is only my fourth season of primary school engagements. How must poor old Reg feel? Little Reg is re-taking his 'A' levels again, and Little More is preparing for hers; preparing for a better class of unemployment, as Reg puts it. He first crossed swords with the education system at his son's playgroup—something about time-sharing an inflatable duck. He lost that match, or maybe it was a draw: the duck got a puncture. It was the sandwich campaign that gave him his first taste of victory; we celebrate the thirteenth anniversary later this year. Little Reg started it. He couldn't be doing with school dinners, or rather, he didn't mind them as long as he wasn't required to eat them—this was in the days of the two-course, luke-warm, mandatory school menu. He wasn't the only one: by and large the under-tens aren't programmed for broad beans, greens, semolina, cabbage and custard, without which school meals were unthinkable.

Little Reg's school got round this impasse by employing dragon dinner ladies to stand over the backsliders, until every scrap had disappeared from their plates. The dragons made the mistake of assuming an empty plate equalled a full stomach, and—like Colditz guards—underestimating the resourcefulness of their victims. The sly ones managed to disperse inedible bits under the table and trample them into the drugget, or secrete them in paper bags, or handkerchiefs and pockets—socks and shoes, even. Little Reg was either too honest or too unimaginative for that; instead he had daily confrontations with one dragon after another, choking and gagging on diced carrots, gristle and greens, until he was sent off to the playground in disgrace—and a drizzle of tears. His indignant father finally decided enough was enough, and decreed that his man-child should henceforth eat sandwiches. The first time he sat down in the hall and took out his little sarnie box, however, he was hauled up before the headmistress for infringing regulations: there was no provision for independent provisions on council premises. Not only that, but the staff couldn't and wouldn't pander to ridiculous fads and fancies; it messed up dinner duties, encouraged indiscipline—not to mention mice—and upset the caretaker; was, in short, the first step on the road to social chaos.

Here was a challenge to gladden Red Reg's heart. He composed a searing letter in which the words 'outrage', 'authoritarian', 'rigid' and 'uncaring' figured prominently. An abrasive interview followed, during which the headmistress tried to lecture him on dietetics. 'I did my

National Service in the Catering Corps,' he said grimly. (Most of it was spent fiddling the accounts in the sergeants' mess, but she wasn't to know that.) The upshot was, that the 'outrageous', 'rigid' head agreed to provide alternative dining accommodation in a stock cupboard, on condition that the dinner drop-out left no crumbs, and ate in solitary confinement, to prevent him corrupting the rest of the school. She'd mistaken her man: the idea of martyrdom appealed to Reg instantly.

'You're on,' he said.

'It seems a high price to pay for a sandwich,' she suggested.

'No price is too high if our liberties are in question,' he replied (Reg loses all sense of proportion when he's being sincere).

'You're occupying that stock-cupboard in the cause of freedom,' he explained to his son later. Little Reg didn't seem too happy about becoming a legend in his own lunch time. 'Every bit of peanut butter sandwich will be a blow for civil rights,' said his father.

'I don't like peanut butter,' Little Reg protested. Reg ignored him and turned to me.

'He'll learn a lesson in that stock cupboard they'll never teach him in the classroom. Young as he is, this boy is taking a stand against the common class enemy.' Little Reg perked up a bit:

'Which class, Dad? Miss Roker's or Miss Tremlow's?'

'Reg,' I said, 'don't kid yourself. I've been a teacher, and I'm telling you. From the school's point of view, you're just another middle-class trouble-maker.' Poor old Reg went white.

'My old man was a docker in the West India,' he squeaked.

'Exactly,' I told him, 'It's always the converts who become zealots.'

Four months later, though, I had to take it all back. That small, bewildered boy sitting in a stock cupboard, with only two slices of Hovis and a banana for company, was the start of one of the liveliest sandwich lunch clubs in South East London. It was also the start of the boy's career as a con-man of great charm and cunning; to this day his father is putty in his hands—he learned his lesson all right.

'You don't understand politics,' says Reg, kindly. 'Show the masses the way and they will rise in support.'

I object that twenty-five little mixed juniors were hardly the masses.

'Percentage-wise, that's the equivalent of three point five per cent of voters, enough to swing an election,' he says.

'On a platform of sandwich clubs for all?' I ask. He looks at me, hurt. Then he looks at me again, condescending, magnanimous in victory.

'It's no good, you just don't understand politics . . .' I can't argue with him.

Reg co-opted himself onto the PTA committee on the strength of that sandwich club. Then, the following year, they elected him Chairman, and the year after that, school governor. 'Elected' is putting it a little strongly perhaps; very few parents want to take on these thankless, time-consuming jobs—when they run out of volunteers, vacancies are filled by coercion, conspiracy or accident. Reg was a volunteer, of course. He leaped onto the endless treadmill of committees and subcommittees with enthusiasm: social committee, summer-fair committee, education committee, publicity committee—the titles changed but not the faces. It was basically the same quorum of volunteers under a new name and function. Year after year they gathered together, a harmless fund-raising local mafia with a shrill, confident voice and negligible power; very English, and an ideal stamping-ground for Reg. He beavered away at fêtes and barn dances, and river trips and coach outings, and sponsored walks or swims.

His one true love was PR work. He press-ganged concerned young parents and staff into a whole series of evening surgeries: on maths, modern languages, computer technology, music, art, the cut-backs and the crisis in education. There always is a crisis, by the way; defining the scope and nature of an educational crisis takes so long, it's too late to do anything about it when you've finally decided what it is you ought to do. This was an Augean stable Reg was born to muck-out; his surgeries were well-attended at the primary school. Fifty or sixty mothers and fathers would roll up, hungry for enlightenment, eager to be told their children's outstanding potential was appreciated; shy and rather nervous, most of them, worried that they might—inadvertently—make their private life a little too public. They left the talking to the managerial dad in Buddy Holly glasses, who seemed to know the jargon, and said it all twice. There were occasional descants from a quiet, soulful couple who were anxious for their offspring to be 'stretched'—by the looks of them, they'd snapped in half around the age of four. A far-out graduate ménage in designer jeans and ponchos were the only real dissenting voice. They'd have preferred to send their sprogs to Dartington or the local free school, only it meant giving up holidays in Corsica. But all in all, Chairman Reg packed them off home feeling committed and responsible, comforted by a vague—and probably mistaken—impression that they were stopping the urban rot, which seemed to spread so quickly to less fortunate people's lives.

It was a different story when his son transferred to a

large boys' comprehensive school. The thought of becoming commissar to two thousand parents from every class, caste, race and religion actually brought him out in a rash. He got himself onto a committee in no time, squared his elbows, and settled down for a go at the big stuff. The old-stagers on the PTA welcomed his chutzpah, but questioned his market research. They shook their heads, smiled and sat back and watched, while he crashed head-on into the wall of apathy that surrounds communal life in the suburbs. He survived the shock, and he's still looking for a way round the wall—but he was badly shaken.

Something odd happens to parents when their children stop being juniors; it's as though these budding taxpayers and citizens had become such a burden to them, they'd rather not be reminded of it. Adolescents are disenfranchised adults with king-size problems that can only get worse—parental togetherness merely underlines how much worse they could get. Better not go to school meetings, then; better stay at home and watch telly, or slip down to the boozer, or paper the back bedroom, and forget it. The managerial dad in specs, the soulful couple, and the designer jeans combo, they might have clung on to the bitter end, but they've made other arrangements in the private sector by now.

Poor Reg, a tribune rejected by the plebs; he has to rely on me or his fellow committee members to appreciate his eloquence, now.

'Parents don't seem to realise,' he says. 'Birth, school and National Insurance—that's the Holy Trinity here in Britain. You have to be born—supposing you want to be here at all—you have to go to school, you have to have a DHSS number; nothing else is obligatory. You can go your own way: into the nick, on the game, round the bend, to hell and back. What's the matter with today's parents?' he asks. 'They can't *ignore* school. God almighty, we spend fourteen-point-six-six per cent recurring of our lives there.'

'Does that include truancy?' I ask him.

'You're missing the point as usual,' he says. 'We're eating the nation's seedcorn. Like a tuppenny bag of chips.'

Reg is very good at finding social or cultural reasons for his own failures. He blames Baden-Powell personally for his bad posture—the strain of keeping his Scout hat and socks straight give him a list. He blames Marshal Goering and Herbert Morrison for his bad game of table tennis—staring through the grille of HM's air-raid shelter during the Blitz distorted his vision. He'll argue from the particular to the general until he drops, whereas most of the parents he wants to reach are only too happy to go contrariwise. They'll flock to school in droves for a confidential chat about their particular Janet or John's progress. At the place I used to teach we ran huge forty-ring circuses several times a year—straight out of Kafka. The main hall was crammed with small tables arranged according to academic subject, around which parent and teacher debated Janet or John's strengths and weaknesses, while other parents waited their turn in orderly queues, clutching itineraries that directed them onwards to other tables and yet more teachers. A four-hour procession of strange faces, low voices, smiles, frowns, pleasure and gloom. The nearest thing to it would be travelling third class from Calais to Vladivostok in the 1890s.

En route round the hall the visitors caught tantalising snatches of other people's dramas, with or without the main protagonist—I mean Janet or John. The wise child stayed away and let the big guns exhaust their ammunition. 'I can't understand it, Miss Pringle, she's so quiet at home.' The wise child knew better than to confuse her classroom and domestic roles. As far as I could see, parents seemed to accept the need for this occasion; teachers submitted to it reluctantly, but they submitted. Very few of either would have come out on a cold night to discuss Education with a big 'E' or inverted commas. Reg reckons this proves his theory that the English are by nature undemocratic, and always were.

'They prefer to be ruled by committees who bother them as little as possible,' he complains, 'oligarchies they can give the chop to now and then. We're a nation of closet sado-masochists.'

I remind him he drew a good crowd for his seminars on sex-education, discipline and public examinations.

'That's what I'm saying,' he says. 'Sado-masochists.'

'They'd come along to see their kids in a concert or a play,' I suggest.

'You have to make the cast bigger than the audience to get a full house,' he says angrily.

Any man who buys thirty shares in the Draw Club to keep it going, and is then criticised for winning too many prizes, a man like that has a right to be angry. Venting his anger isn't easy, either; he feels inhibited in committee. The regular members are mostly jolly middle-aged ladies with afternoons and evenings—and energy—to spare. They belong to the generation who had no careers or gave them up for child-rearing, and are now seeking an outlet for their unused talents. Reg is providing the outlet. 'Listen,' he says, 'if they gave a modest grant to all the PTA ladies in the country, the government and the rest of us could knock off and go home. They'd set the economy to rights, reduce unemployment and stop the arms race, simply by nationalising bring-and-buy sales and whist drives.' His admiration is reciprocated: at school barn dances and discos Reg is in constant demand as a partner. Big More his wife, who has a malicious sense of humour, refuses to accompany him—for fear of making the ladies jealous, she says. My heart went out to him; the organisation and sweated labour involved in a PTA function is bad enough, without the indignity of sexual harassment. When he asked me to act as chaperone-cum-aide-de-camp at the next social, I couldn't very well refuse.

It was fixed for a Friday night, but on Thursday evening we had to go down and manhandle a barrel of real-ale into the drama hut, to give it time to settle. When we arrived we found the brewery had delivered it to the wrong side of the school.

'Let's wait for the rest of the lads,' I advised.

'They can't make it,' said Reg.

So we began rolling the real-ale down to the drama hut. By some oversight, barrels are made without brakes or steering, and we accidentally knocked over the caretaker's bike and buckled his front wheel. We shoved it to the back of the bike shed, so he would blame the kids, and carried on rolling. The drama hut was locked, however, and after an argument, Reg persuaded me to fetch the key from the caretaker's house. The latter was very suspicious.

'You seen a bike?'

'No,' I lied.

'There'll be murder done if I don't find it.'

I wondered what crime he'd commit when he *did* find it.

The caretaker looked me over. 'Are you macramé or yoga?'

'No, PTA.'

When we'd pushed the barrel into the hut, we played double-rupture-or-split and hoisted it onto some cradles. Then Reg couldn't find a bung to fit it, and went off to borrow one from a bloke in the Labour Party. 'Find the mallet while I'm gone,' he said. 'It's behind the radiators somewhere.' Trying to disengage the mallet from a mess of rope, I inadvertently released a net of balloons the art department had hung up, together with a load of weird decorations that looked like mad bats. Before I could hoist the net and the balloons back up again, two of the Boys' Brigade from the hut next door strolled in, and grabbed half-a-dozen while I wasn't looking. I thought it best not to mention that to Reg; he was under enough pressure already. While he broached the barrel, I turned off the radiators to keep the beer at the right temperature. 'That's that,' he said, locking the hut, 'long as the drama department keep their elbows to themselves.'

Next day I rejoined Reg in the hut at four o'clock. He'd taken two hours off work to get things started, and was already wrestling with a gas pump and a keg of lager, surrounded by crates of light and brown, cases of wine and six jolly ladies in perms and aprons. They were laying out food and glasses on trestle tables covered with paper. 'Who's your friend?' one of them asked Reg, and patted me on the bottom. This is going to be a long evening, I thought.

'Stick up the opticals,' said Reg.

'Pardon?' I said.

'Opticals for the spirits.' He pointed to a drawer, but they weren't there . . . 'That bugger in the business studies department has nabbed them, he runs a club on the side. Slip down to the Duke's Head, say Reg says it's happened again, and could George oblige.'

George duly obliged, and I got the opticals clamped to a shelf. Then Reg set me to pinning up the licence and inventing a profitable tariff, with everything rounded up to the nearest 10p for convenience. After that the band arrived: two guitars, an accordion, a sax, a drummer who was already the worse for drink, and half a ton of sound system. Reg waved at the power points and made for the gents, to change into his costume, he said.

'Costume?' I asked.

'Yes, got yours?' He nodded at the mad bat decorations. 'It's a Transylvanian evening, didn't you notice?'

'Oh, you must have a costume, everybody does,' trilled the jolly ladies.

'Fix him up, girls,' ordered Reg. 'Anything ghoulish will do, he's half-way there already.'

There was no time to register a protest. The jolly ladies laughed and whipped me off to a backroom, bubbling over with pent-up talent and latent power. There they wrapped me in a white table-cloth, powdered my face with ghostly talc, and drew mascara rings under my eyes.

'They're a lovely blue,' said a lady, 'is your wife coming?'

'Yes, both of them as a matter of fact—' I was panicking a bit by now but it seemed bad manners not to wear the costume. Round about then there was a fiendish howl-back from the speakers, and the lights fused. Dashing over to the band to help, I collided with the percussion section in the murk, and grabbed at the tipsy drummer for support. With a cry, he jerked away from me, crashed through the emergency exit doors, and hurled himself into the twilight outside.

'I'm supposed to be a ghoul,' I explained.

'Don't ever do that to a whisky man again,' he said . . . Reg groped his way to the fuse-box, half dressed as a one-armed police chief.

'I do like to see a man in uniform,' whispered a jolly lady.

'And out of it,' roared another. They collapsed into each other's arms, shrieking hysterically.

Three quarters of an hour before the off, a quartet of fathers arrived to bar-tend: sturdy, hairy-armed, well-shaved, monosyllabic men, who took an instant dislike to my ghoul get-up and decided to ignore me. After which, they sampled the ale with a far-away look, nodded at Reg with grudging approval, grinned at the ladies, and gave them a perfunctory tickle to establish their credentials. Then they donned Hallowe'en masks specially bought from the joke shop, folded their arms and stood around like gargoyles, gloomily discussing their children's 'O' level prospects. The drummer lurched over to collect 'house' drinks for the band. 'Thirsty work,' he said—unconvincingly.

'Where's the bottle openers?' asked a gargoyle suddenly. 'Call this a bar?'

'My friend will get some,' said Reg, pointing in my direction. 'He won't be long . . .'

I doffed my white sheet, drove down to the local off-licence and strode in. 'Bottle openers,' I demanded, 'It's urgent.' The proprietor stared at me strangely.

'Balls,' he said, 'you've had enough already.' I caught sight of my reflection in a display cabinet, white-faced and hollow-eyed.

'It's a school fancy-dress party,' I told him. 'We're desperate.'

'I should think you are,' he said, but he sold me three openers.

When I got back the guests were arriving and the band was busking 'Strangers in the Night'. The jolly ladies were now decked out in bright décolleté dresses, and holding a cantilever competition—there was enough flesh on show to satisfy a mausoleum of vampires. Every second male guest was wearing a black coat and clip-on fangs, which they had to remove every time they ate or drank. The drama hut began to take on the appearance of a dental massacre. There were a couple of Frankenstein monsters, an Igor or two, and the science department took the easy option, arriving *en masse* in white coats. The headmaster made a grand entry in a braided tunic and shako—nobody had the nerve to tell him it was Transylvania, not Ruritania. When a fully-fledged ghoul arrived with a wig and green eye-shadow, I took refuge in the backroom and devoted myself to washing glasses; a huge pile was already waiting.

Working behind the bar was too hairy for me. The four gargoyles went at it as if the punters were issuing a challenge to their manhood instead of ordering drinks. There was the regular clunk and jingle of empty bottles and cans, the tinkle and crunch of dropped glass crushed under foot. I was reminded of the torpedo room in a submarine at action stations. A heavy pall of real-ale vapour hung in the air and spread through the drama hut, like a hang-over waiting to descend. If the gargoyles hadn't pushed the hallowe'en masks to the back of their heads they'd have suffocated—it made them seem more like gargoyles than ever.

The black coats, fangs and Igor humps were now laid aside for greater ease in drinking and dancing—the bosoms of the jolly ladies turned puce with the excitement of it all. The one who liked uniforms seized Reg for a whirl round the dance floor. When I tried to come to his rescue, the one who liked blue eyes caught me by my soggy ghoul sheet and whisked me off as well. 'Do ghouls do it?' she asked huskily, breathing gin and orange over me. 'Never,' I said, 'they're past it.' On our second circuit relief came, in the shape of the lager pump exploding over the gargoyles. As Reg and I panted up, they were feverishly turning off valves and lunging with mops. The resemblance to a submarine was now irresistible.

'Up periscope!' I yelled, illogically.

'Take him outside,' said a gargoyle, 'he's pissed.' One of the ladies rushed to oblige.

'Women and children first,' I cried, and escaped back to the washing up.

'It must be time for the buffet,' said Reg, wearily.

A few minutes later the band stuttered and died, and a horde of hungry Transylvanians descended on the chicken salad, cheese, pâté and trifle the ladies had laid on. A trail of edible debris began to appear amongst the spilt cigarette ash, broken glass and dead wine bottles.

'We want this lot cleaned up for *Midsummer Night's Dream* rehearsals on Monday,' said the well-appointed, supercilious ghoul—who, of course, was the drama specialist. Reg picked up a pair of discarded fangs and assessed the size of the problem.

'Blood transfusions would have been a lot cleaner,' he said, in a rare resort to fantasy.

I leaned against a radiator and looked round at the seepage and spillage. My soggy ghoul gown slipped, and—like an idiot—I tried to steady myself on the rope that released the balloons. They floated gently down against the thermal of rising hot air, and the diners snatched at them delightedly. The drama hut was filled with staccato explosions as they stamped and sat upon them, screaming with laughter, littering the floor with the bright red, green, yellow and blue skins, and adding to the scrub of refuse.

'You've wrecked the grand finale,' said Reg.

'I've enhanced the interval a treat,' I pointed out. He closed his eyes.

'At our VE street party in West Ham,' he said, 'we constructed a table forty yards long. Three hundred of us sat down together. We were at it twelve hours non-stop, eating, drinking, singing and dancing. And I put my hand under Ethel Partridge's blouse, when her mother went upstairs with the rent man . . .'

I nudged him. 'The back of the bike shed is free, Reg. And there's bags of talent—' I was thinking of the jolly ladies. Reg shook his head.

'There's no passion or poetry in you—how about tomorrow morning?'

'Do what?' I asked.

'We usually clear up the morning after,' he said.

'I'm afraid I've got an important appointment,' I told him. He seemed doubtful.

'You're unemployed . . .'

'Only on paper.'

'What's that supposed to mean?'

'There's the children to think of, the washing, the shopping, the milkman. I'm a househusband, you forget.'

He sat down and sighed. 'I'm a chairman, I have no excuses.'

'Why do you do it Reg?' I asked sympathetically.

'Because I believe in demystifying the system.' He glared at the Transylvanians as they waded into their desserts. A jolly lady tripped across to him, toying wantonly with a trifle.

'Schools were never like this when I was a girl,' she simpered.

'No,' said Reg.

Recently his wife began tempting him to transfer their daughter to a quiet school in Chislehurst. It stands in extensive grounds that make it an awkward place to visit after hours. The parents concentrate on clapping at open day and holding the occasional cheese and wine. When I accused him of selling out, he looked away and mumbled, something about going where no socialist dared to tread, carrying the fight to the foe.

'It'll be a short, sharp fight,' I told him. 'Your daughter leaves school in two years.'

'A five-year plan changed the face of Soviet Industry,' he said.

'They had some help from Stalin and the NKVD', I reminded him . . . He'll need to resurrect both before Chislehurst turns Red.

8 *Cheapsakes*

The old shoe shop round the corner has closed. The glass shelves in the window are stripped bare: a few faded price tickets remind you of bargains no longer available. I mourn the passing of the unpretentious, under-stocked, local tradesman, smug and self-satisfied as he often was. The amount of choice in a large modern store confuses me, and the snazzy interior designs and multiple mirrors do something to my alpha waves—definitely. They're meant to, of course; a distracted shopper is more likely to surrender to a sudden, irrational, spending spree. Ten minutes in the old shoe shop, and you were provided with neat, comfortable unfashionable footwear, that lasted you and yours for years: desert boots, brogues, Oxfords; and solid kiddy sandals that even—amazing, this—survived to be second or third hand, fourth in a jumble sale. My regrets are motivated by thrift as well as nostalgia, but a genuine sadness comes over me when I peer behind that CLOSING DOWN sign, and see the back-to-back rows of dark bentwood chairs, scattered in disorder; the stock reduced to one broken shoe box, and a crooked shoe horn on a string. The three rhomboid footstools stand like headstones, commemorating four or five generations of well-shod feet, a good number of whom marched away to two World Wars, and never trod a footstool again. Saddest sight of all is a pair of portable library steps, leaning against the rows of empty shelves. Four steps up, four steps down: and nowhere to go—in either direction.

A good local shoe shop and a good library used to have a lot in common: you went in, you sat down, and a knowledgeable assistant brought you a selection of sensible, leather-bound works to choose from. You thought about weight, size and quality; wondered whether you could get into them, and went home with the ones that fitted and suited you best. As time passed, you got more and more used to them, until eventually they were part of your life, part of yourself, almost. Civilised folk find it hard to keep their feet on the ground, you notice. Our shoes and boots keep in touch, make contact for us, do an awful lot of our living—I wouldn't be in *his* shoes, we say. They're our stand-ins, our vicars here on earth. And books are just the same, shoes for the mind when it goes out walking. Boots and books—that's all civilisation *is*, really. Well, I've heard worse definitions before now, and much longer ones, too. Now I think back, the footwear trade must have been well aware of this dualism. Shop assistants were very often critics as well. They'd make a thorough analysis of the work in hand: style, structure, content, cost and likely public appeal; then they'd retire politely and allow you to form your own opinion in peace. It's very different nowadays. Shoe shops or sex shops, it makes no odds. Seven out of ten South London sales-persons regard customers as inconvenient, inefficient hiccups in the consumption process. Their ideal client would have a mouth like a Volkswagen boot, and a cash-dispenser where his right arm is.

Contemporary shoe stores seem to have forgotten their civilising mission entirely, and entered a new Dark Age. The relaxed library atmosphere has gone, the shelves and shoe boxes are generally hidden in the stock room; instead, you're confronted by gaunt metal racks, on which families of unpaired boots and shoes are impaled. You think of Hitchcock, or the locker room at a wooden-leg convention. When you point to a shoe, an assistant looks disapproving, but fetches a pair from stock, and dangles them before you, limply. The effort seems to have drained her—it's usually a she, I'm afraid. Her body goes slack, her eyes flicker round the store shiftily, as if the stock room was actually full of contraband, and she expected customs and excise any minute: bootlegging, you're nicked. Attempt to involve her in your choice, and she grunts and squirms, as though you'd made an improper suggestion. If you decide not to buy, she switches into zombie mode and sleepwalks back to the stock room; if you *do* buy, she only dumps your shoes at the cash desk and sidles off, disinterested. You begin to think it's personal, and wish you had changed your socks. The cash desk is manned—it's often a man—by a grovelling wrapper-upper and money-changer, a feeble effort to compensate for the girl's indifference. In any case, he spoils the effect by trying to sell you over-priced boot polish and shoe trees. And did those feet, indeed . . .

My friend Reg puts it all down to the embourgeoisification of the workers. The cheerful, attentive sales assistants of yore now pass exams and head off towards lusher pastures, leaving the poor old lumpen-proletariat to cope as best they can. I'm not convinced, because the worst offenders are part-time assistants in supermarkets; and a fair proportion of them are the elite he's talking about, dabbling in retail distribution for pin money. They shovel the produce down the conveyor belt like dustbin men in a hurry. The staff and stuff of life that fellaheen, kibbutzim, harijan and peons have sweated over for years. It flashes by in seconds, unacknowledged, unsung, scarcely a word spoken—unless the price stamp is missing, or the cash register goes on the blink. Deeply irreligious as I am, I can see there's something to be said for Grace at table. Customers are parties to the crime, of course, but you have to let them off with a caution. They've spent ages, and half a pay-packet—or two thirds of a giro cheque—shoving and heaving at their trolleys, in and out the crowd, up and down the loaded aisles and back again, because they've forgotten fish fingers. The common, weekly round puts some of them in a mood for talk and retrospection. I can't go into a supermarket without meeting at least two old acquaintances who are burning to tell me about their operations, or how they stood bail for their eldest, or wrote the car off, or caught a bug in Portugal. I wish the staff could be brought into the act somehow; the new microprocessor at the check-out ought to give them the time, if they had the inclination. But it wasn't invented for that. It's there to help you pay up, and get the hell out of it as soon as possible.

I'm beginning to think and talk like my old granny, for whom nothing ever got better, and everything changed for the worst. A figure of fun she was, and now she's bequeathed her bad habits to me—I wasn't due to inherit for years, I'm not even middle-aged yet. The legacy will have to be disavowed, or my daughters will disown me altogether. They already make me feel like the Albert Memorial. Mind you, the under-elevens have a very hazy sense of history. The other day daughter number one asked if I used to watch the Kaiser on television when I was her age. So you see, the incentive to come to grips with change and built-in obsolescence is there, if only they hadn't sneaked up and put a head-lock on me before I was ready—change and built-in obsolescence, not my daughters; although they do it, too. And children are change and obsolescence personified, amongst a thousand other things.

Fifteen years ago Penge High Street was still—unmistakably—a prosperous Victorian village, with bakelite knobs on, perhaps. It was the parson's nose of London, not immediately appetising, but nourishing nonetheless. At one end, the windows of the watermen's almshouse winked across at the flourishing street market; at the other, the Edwardian police station kept a watchful eye on the excesses of the Odeon and Co-op. Now the dwindling company of street traders gather round the entrance to a car-park and poky shopping precinct; a thin, grey line, watching the motorists drive by them, to pick up another bulk load of disposable goodies—the ones who can't make it to Croydon or Bromley, that is. The Co-op has given up co-operating, the other big shops are closed or closing; the Odeon was de-odeonised to a Bingo parlour yonks since. And the police: the police are probably too busy chasing flying pickets, or tapping phones, to notice they're now keeping watch on a battery farm, not a suburb. If you don't believe me, just take a peek at a cut-price emporium in Croydon or Bromley during normal trading hours. You're bound to find some Penge folk, huddling together under the warm neon lights, laying their hard-earned nest eggs in corporate tills. Cheap-cheap, they squawk. If I remember rightly, the word originally meant 'to buy'; to buy a bargain, obviously, or the meaning wouldn't have changed. Selling and buying implied haggling, a relationship of sorts; in these days of standard prices and standard goods, relationships are uneconomic—only the ghost of a haggle lingers. Cheap has become more or less synonymous with disposable, I suppose. When our rulers, elders and betters abdicate in favour of King Silicon, they will do so because the merry monarch has the power to make people as disposable as the products they buy. The throw-away electorate is the solution to every politician's problems, and the answer to all his dreams—or hers, of course.

If I'm honest, I've never been one for shopping on the grand scale, not since I caught my sister's rabbit in the escalator at Gamage's, when I was ten—a furry rabbit, you understand, a toy one. I'm not blind to the advantages and economies that come with increased size. Honest public lending companies must secure themselves against bankruptcy in times like these; they're not to blame for the fall in manufacturing output and so forth—at least, I don't think they are. Yet I still can't work up much sympathy for them, I'm liable to shrink and dwindle—like Alice—in department stores. The larger the store, the greater the shrinkage. My wife has no patience with this little weakness, but I can usually bribe my eight-year-old daughter to create a diversion and keep our shopping expeditions short; a milk-shake might shorten one by thirty minutes, for instance. If small retail outlets go on disappearing at the present rate, though, I shall have to have recourse to mail-order catalogues. Up until now I've thought of them more as fiction than commerce. (By the by, I've got nothing against Croydon or Bromley shopping centres, or their poor relation at Penge. They're all very well in their place, but there's no keeping them within bounds. They're like those urban reservoirs that draw on rivers and streams fifty miles from any city. The retail river beds of Penge are beginning to dry up fast, I can tell you.)

We've hung on to our Woolworth's. I don't know how—they've been dropping like dehydrated dinosaurs all round South London. A dead Woollies is a disturbing sight; they leave cruel gashes in any high street. Those long, white-washed windows, like screens round hospital beds. We have plenty of other casualties, however, respectable established concerns, a lot of them. They hide their shame behind blanked-out façades, and stare wall-eyed at the traffic. Some will undergo cosmetic surgery pretty soon, I expect. Marauding bands of leaseholders are on the rampage. They aim to give punters the come-on by a quick nose job on the shop-fronts—ponces managing clapped-out tarts. It's getting difficult to keep track, the amount of frantic dismantling, re-assembling and refurbishing that goes on.

The hardware store is a classic example. Once it overflowed with indispensables. They spilled out on to the pavement, a tidal wave of zinc baths, besoms, coconut mats, chicken-wire, dog-baskets, incinerators, funnels and lavatory plungers. The interior was heavily perfumed, with paraffin, hard yellow soap, firelighters, hemp, candles, linseed oil, and a pungent metallic tang from the boxes of screws, nails, hacksaw blades and brass curtain rods—so powerful, your nostrils flared. The store extended the full length of the building, creating a dim, windowless cavern amidshops. Its proprietor was a grey-skinned troglodyte in pepper-and-salt overalls; he seemed to merge with his wares like an old lizard on the rocks.

It was plastic that did for him, I think; he could never seem to merge with that. Chain-stores cloned new varieties of pastel-shaded baths and baskets too quickly and cheaply for him to adapt. After a few years' struggle he gave in, and kicked his last bucket. His musty catacomb stood empty for about five years, but you could still snuff its steely, tarry fragrance through the letter-box—if, like me, you had nothing better to do. Then the batten and cladding boys invaded: they gutted, tore down, rewired, turned darkness into light—fit-up theatre really, not interior design at all. The old lizard's habitat was transformed into a conti-board and perspex clip-joint, offering up-market bathroom suites in aubergine, buttercup and burgundy. There was a jacuzzi on display in the window, babbling lasciviously to itself, twenty-four hours a day. Gossip has it that the glamorous widow across the road had one installed in her bedroom. I'd like to know where these rumours start—in her bedroom, presumably.

Apart from the widow there are very few out-and-out sybarites south of Clapham Common. The bath-tub vendors had nothing to do but sit around and fiddle with their brochures, waiting for someone with a couple of thousand quid to chuck away; their enterprise was always stronger on optimism than good taste or judgement. Penge as a body couldn't warm to jacuzzis. Old ladies and gentlemen would stop and stare through the window at them sheepishly, imagining them to be a new-fangled marital aid, perhaps, or a contraceptive device—which I'm told they sometimes are. 'Thinking of investing in one?' I asked the retired railwayman, when I caught him at it one day. 'Useful for bathing the dog,' he said, and walked off in a huff. A few months later the business folded: the jacuzzis and bathroom suites were taken back to the depot, leaving ugly tidemarks along the wainscot where they had stood.

If I had to lay bets on the next owners, I'd say a building society or an insurance brokers—or an estate agents. The number of their offices you see in a district is probably a good measurement of urban decay. They're architectural polyfilla, they stop up the holes in run-down high streets, without plugging the gaps in goods and services; they've got nothing to sell except money, basically, like the banks. One day, perhaps, someone will mint a currency with denominations you can eat, wear, sleep or sit on: then everything will be for the best in the best of all possible markets . . .

If the shop isn't converted into an office, I'd put money

each way on fast-foods, boutiques or antiques. There's a two-hundred-yard stretch of road near here that has eleven take-away restaurants—three Chinese, two kebab, three hamburger, two Indian, one fish-and-chips—plus seven boutiques, and six so-called antique shops (my friend Reg says they're full of the old tat his mum threw away when the council moved her to a maisonette). These new retail trends must mean something. Perhaps Pengeians are so busy flogging the family's old tat, or buying some other family's, they haven't got time to cook; and if they're simultaneously rushing around trying to sell or buy a house, and reinsure themselves, well, that's just asking for an identity crisis. Which would explain the boutiques: instant, ready-to-wear identities in fashionable colours are their speciality. I've diagnosed a new medical condition—call it Penge Syndrome. An essential part of the treatment will be pleated skirts and chop suey. The local Health Service will be stretched to breaking-point—they're already closing hospitals as though Boot's had the elixir of life on offer.

But I mustn't mock. These changes in neighbourhood spending habits are a very serious matter, my Uncle Jim will vouch for that. Come five o'clock one September Saturday, I'll suddenly remember I've forgotten his birthday present again, and he'll never forgive me—again. My wife had hopes of his Royal Worcester dinner-service when he pops off, but I think I've blown it. Up until a few years ago I could always dash round to the menswear shop, and pick up a present there. Five minutes away, door to door, and five decades once you were *through* the door. They still had suspenders and flannel pyjamas in stock; gaberdine trousers, homburgs, white mufflers, braces that really braced. The manager sported a toothbrush moustache, and wore a watch-chain, a rotarian tie-pin and a handkerchief in his breast-pocket. At the word of command, he'd parade a squad of Uncle Jim-type gloves, scarves or cardigans on the glass counter. Then he'd look out of the window, cough and say: 'Chilly for the time of year, sir.' He acquired his style from cinema butlers, I should think. He survived the 'sixties and early 'seventies by shaving off his moustache and reluctantly stocking up with denim, but he went to the wall in '79, about the time turn-ups starting coming back. It must've been very disheartening after all his efforts. The place is a gold and silver exchange now: you have to ring for admittance. It's not a shop at all, it's a bank vault with visiting hours.

The most revealing case of transretailism—to coin a phrase—was the industrial clothing shop. It occupied a commanding position on a main road, but it made no attempt to advertise or attract customers. The exterior was painted cocoa-brown—so was the interior; the windows were piled with bundles of overalls, aprons, and boiler suits in strong blues and browns. Inside there were more of the same on racks, keeping company with rows of knobbly black and brown industrial boots. It could have been a headless group portrait by Magritte. When I was going through my Chairman Mao phase, I had a plan to buy a whole outfit there, but my current girlfriend, who was into beads and decorated kaftans, thought we would clash at parties. Industrial clothing wasn't of much practical use to teachers of English, admittedly; in fact, I'm sure the headmaster would have seen it as political bias and sent me home. But the gear in that shop exerted a strange attraction over me at the time—so functional, so uncompromising, so necessary. By appointment, tailors to the real world. Those overalls and boiler suits were the disguise I needed to escape from the relentless self-abuse of the 'sixties—I don't mean it literally, although some of us may have gone blind for a while . . . Of course, I was deluding myself. We weren't to know it, but the industrial clothing shop, and the industries it clothed, were on the way out as fast as swinging London. Opening hours grew progressively shorter, then it closed for two days a week, while the lessee took a part-time job; which gradually became full-time. And that was the end—or rather, the beginning.

Within two months—like Hamlet's mother's wedding, and twice as shocking—it magicked itself into a little bistro, which then compounded the insult by flaunting wrought-iron tables and Martini umbrellas on the pavement. The old cocoa-brown interior turned green and gold, blossomed into swagged velour curtains and hunting prints. The effect is *entente cordiale* Paris, although I'm not sure about the intention—more *cordiale* than Paris, perhaps, and very weak on *entente.* It's presided over by two laconic gay lads, who are fond of their food, and even fonder of cooking it. Of course, you pay for their pleasure; and the menu is limited, not to say handicapped, but it's good enough to seduce an unwaged metropolitan househusband like me, with a little financial assistance from my wife and friends. I'm a minor patron, you could say, whereas I only patronised the clothing shop in my fantasies. My friend Reg rubbed salt into this wound only last week. We were eating at the bistro with our superior halves, when he suddenly went all morose and, glaring round at the velour curtains, began speculating about what the previous customers would have made of such decadence—the stokers, fitters, boilermen and other industrial workmen. Guilt drove me to the attack.

'Don't worry, the workers are loving it,' I said, and pointed to a local gas-fitter I knew, who was tucking into tournedos opposite. 'He's not about to unite and throw off his chains, not before the blackcurrant fool,' I said. 'And if he did, there'd be someone round from the job centre to try them on before he got to the cheese. The masses aren't half as massive as they used to be, Reg.' This was a long speech by my standards.

'Have you finished?' he asked.

'Yes,' I said, 'shall I get you the bill?' Reg took out his American Express card, assumed a pained expression, and started a long whinge, about how he used to get dinner for a bob in Mudie's Eel and Pie at East Ham, and how there were no communal eating places left any more.

He was wrong about that. Big John's ice-cream parlour and snack-bar is only fifty yards from the bistro. The rock of Penge, unshaken by the tide of shop-closures and retail bankruptcies. Big John no doubt claims credit for that—a hard-nosed man of business if ever there was. Personally, I think his soft-nosed wife and her crew of amateur shop-girls are responsible. In their hands every customer becomes a comic crisis requiring their undivided attention. This is not only good entertainment, it's oddly reassuring and restful. What with the clinical whiteness and gleaming chrome, you walk out feeling more like a restored patient than a customer—a free topping of librium on every tub and cornet, and no side-effects, apart from another visit to the dentist. Over the years, Big John's inessential business has become an indispensable public amenity. The atmosphere is more like a Viennese café than you'd think possible from a quick glance at the décor: genuine English Naff, but so naïve and artless, it disarms the scoffers and critics. The clientele is drawn from every conceivable class and trade. Maybe a hint of Neapolitan vulgarity does the trick—Big John is a third generation immigrant from Sorrento. A suggestion of foreign-ness always gives the English licence to forget themselves.

People walk into that ice-cream parlour who wouldn't be seen dead in McDonald's. I've observed the wife of a senior *Times* journalist drink a milk-shake in there, unaccompanied (wives of *Times* journalists are well-known to be as discriminating as Mansion House toastmasters); I've watched a professor of aeronautics drink chocolate, a suffragan bishop take tea and strudel, an up and coming rock-star polish off a banana split. They look mighty pleased with their own condescension, of course: they aerosol the common man with repeated indulgent smiles. The common man is tolerant and refuses to be compromised—English Naff couldn't exist as a genre without him, and he knows it; or *she* knows it: the customers are seventy per cent female. Harassed mothers slipping noisy toddlers a mickey-finn lollipop; elderly widows freaking out on a second chocolate sundae; schoolgirls sucking down nicotine and coke, and eyeing themselves in the mirror, to see how provocative they can look.

There is also a gang of ageing regulars, cheery, fly-brained, geriatric ladies, for whom Big John's—open seven days a week—is sole refuge and public entertainment. 'The Senior Citizens' Club is no use to me,' says one of them, 'It's full of daft old women and dirty old men.' This is a gross libel on the Senior Citizens' Club, but old Gwen can't stand being organised, however gently. She arrives around noon and stays till two, eating a succession of small snacks, as and when the fancy takes her. Raspberry Surprise followed by egg-on-toast, followed by walnut whip, followed by bacon butty, followed by pineapple milk-shake and pork scratchings —the whole washed down with cups of bovril and milkless tea. If they ever get old Gwen into the Senior Citizens' Club she'll drive them crazy. During the course of this binge she'll smoke three or four cigarettes, and regale the counter and customers with details of her itinerary that day, or the day before, or the other week, and her plans for a fortnight hence. These involve trips to alleged friends in forgotten pleasure resorts like Canvey Island or Pitsea marshes; incredibly complex journeys, in which the route numbers of buses take on the importance of a safe combination, or a diplomatic cipher. If she actually goes on one of these mythical expeditions it provides her with a monologue that lasts a month in daily instalments: a monologue—she doesn't require responses, or attention, even, simply a captive audience. Just as well probably, the part-time counter staff—frail students and petite housewives—need to save their strength for the ice-cream scoops. Deceptively simple instruments, they call for the forearms of a navvy and the wrists of a Boston Strangler.

Three or four times a week Big John's is given a breath of Montmartre: two lovers use it for afternoon assignations. They sit in a corner, or behind a pillar, and spin a little cocoon of oblivion around themselves for forty-five minutes. She feeds him her cheese omelette and tutti-frutti: he reciprocates with his baked beans and chip-mint-choc—spooning and 'spooning' at one and the same time, very cost-effective. He's a good fourteen stone, built like a wrestler, and she's a spare, athletic blonde, so it's clearly a grooming ritual, not necessity. I think he works in the local health club, and I'm glad I'm not her husband. The latter can't be very partial to ice-cream, whoever he is; why else would his unfaithful wife go regularly to Big John's? It's a bit short on moonlight and roses, for all its remarkable qualities—unless the lovers have a passion for ice-cream as well as for each other. I've noticed they work through Big John's range of flavours fairly systematically. Well, why not? Hard-nosed man of business he may be, but he is also a gifted chef glacé; the walls of his shop are festooned with certificates and diplomas from trade fairs and conventions. There's hardly a taste known to Nature he hasn't attempted, from purest white coconut, through red-currant sorbet, to pitch-black liquorice. It looks like the sediment from drains but tastes very good. I wasn't keen on his plum-duff ice-cream, nor the dandelion, and—frankly—his Kiwi-fruit smells like concentrated cleaning fluid. However, the rest of the range is a triumph. If you wanted to carp, you could accuse him of going for surprise rather than delicacy, but that's the secret of his appeal: across the whole spectrum of Penge palates. In matters of taste he's a democrat, although he doesn't know it; his wife may, intuitively at least. Between them they have raised up an ice-cream parlour that survives and thrives through slump and boom. Long may Penge beat a path to its door.

9 *DIY or Die*

The pharmaceutical salesman next door has notched up another victory—very self-satisfied he looks about it, too. I'm talking about his DIY campaign. He attacks home and garden as if they were deadly enemies that had to be subdued and made to conform, whatever the cost; I'm surprised he hasn't painted a row of crossed Black and Deckers on his gable end, like an ace fighter pilot. He only moved in six months ago, but he's already stripped all the doors and the banisters, put vanity units in the bathroom and bedrooms, lagged the loft, built a rockery and dug a fish-pond. His latest triumph is a patio. Four long weekends he laboured, under a blazing sun, spreading a Kalahari of sand beneath a king's ransom of fancy paving stones, and driving his two under-fives to distraction. They wanted to play with the sand, of course, but having twice escaped being crushed under the paving, they were shut up in the kitchen while daddy played on his own. Seen from above, through our lavatory window, with his flapping white shirt-tails and a knotted handkerchief over his head, he looked like an impoverished Penge pharaoh, laying the foundations of his own pyramid. I didn't know whether to envy or pity him, hate him or gloat over him.

His repeated triumphs put my lifetime of painful defeats into cruel perspective; I cannot pick up any kind of tool or implement without some malevolent spirit taking possession of me, mind and body. Wood splits, masonry disintegrates, nails bend, ceilings collapse, wires short-circuit, and vital bits and pieces disappear down gaps in floorboards. The disaster is total, Grecian: I'm Orestes pursued by the fates, murder, madness and chaos are only just around the corner. Forgive me, Messrs Spear and Stanley, Messrs Black, Decker and Braun; a bad workman—an excruciatingly bad workman—I do not blame your tools. This thing is bigger than both of us.

Penge is no place for a DIY drop-out. Walking down the avenue yesterday I counted ten houses undergoing major alterations at the hands of their owners: bare windows, bare light bulbs, bare walls, bare hands banging and scraping. The mere sight of these things turns my stomach over, they're the south col on Everest for me, my North-West passage, rounding the Horn. Orestes should never have gone home to Mum, home is the most dangerous place in the world—there are statistics to prove it. You're more likely to die, be killed, be maimed, be murdered in your own home than anywhere else . . . Or is the strain of isolation getting to me at last? I seem to be the only non-swimmer in an ocean of domestic competence. Local estate agents are actually advertising houses as 'an ideal challenge for the DIY enthusiast'. A fortnight ago the glamorous widow across the way set to and constructed a front porch for herself. Her current handyman and resident lover had sustained a groin injury—up a ladder while he was repairing a fanlight, I hasten to add. She hammered, drilled and re-hung doors without a single oath, one hint of a tear, wearing a bikini, high-heeled golden sandals and faultless manicure. I didn't know where to look—for shame, I mean. In her situation I'd have cursed and sweated, raved and wept, and been led indoors by my wife before I committed a breach of the peace, or did myself some permanent damage.

If you can meet with disaster and disaster—you'll know what it's like to be my wife. Eleven years of marriage to me have made her stoical. But my skin is as thin as ever. Just as I think I've come to terms with my disability, we'll be invited out to a meal by some clever-clogs who has built a brick wall or fitted a kitchen. His—or her—maddening complacency ruins my appetite, takes the edge off my best jokes and brings on a bout of self-loathing that lasts for days. My impediment goes back a long way, you see. At school I was chucked out of woodwork for desecrating a harmless length of two-by-four. They put me at the back of the girls' needlework class, where I spent the time ogling behind my set-books—boys weren't encouraged to sew in Harold Wilson's Britain. The girls cut me dead, naturally. A real man knew how to handle his two-by-four; timber and metal were masculine media. If you couldn't solder, saw and counter-sink there must be a hormone deficiency somewhere. Faced with this conventional wisdom, I gave fate the defiant two fingers, and sentenced myself to twenty years of pointless agony, in an effort to prove my manhood. Nobody seems to *understand*—apart from my wife, who has seen the medical evidence. She's convinced my cack-handedness is congenital, or at least organic: I've got DIY-rosis the way other people have got double-joints or knock-knees. I tried to interest my doctor in this unusual condition; I thought I might make a nice little article in *The Lancet*. But my doctor is a man who spends his days worrying and talking about the Welsh chapel he's converting at weekends. My affliction is not recognised, my struggles ignored. We DIY-rotics are going to have to organise some self-help, like the alcoholics and gamblers: Incompetents Anonymous. We'll also need a national flag-day to pay for our repair bills.

I'm tired of people telling me DIY is easy, common sense

is all you need. My friend Reg is the worst offender: 'If I can do it, anyone can do it,' he says. Certainly, his home is full of crooked shelves, sticky cupboard doors and lop-sided wall-units. They stay where they are and do the job intended for them, however. In our place my pitiful efforts have left a kind of fault-line running through the entire house; seismic disturbances are imminent, every minute of the day. Shelves with missing rawlplugs waiting to capsize; light fittings with loose terminals waiting to explode; curtains with weak runners waiting to collapse; hinges with loose screws waiting to be wrenched off. If the front door bell rings more than four times, every picture in the house is liable to fall down; and the pictures are vital in the sitting room, where they cover up the gaps, bulges and wrinkles in the wallpaper —the ones that the *monstera* and rubber plant don't hide. My wife has a talent for camouflage, fortunately, but she can't conceal the truth from *me.* Waking or sleeping, a seismograph in my brain keeps constant watch. Sometimes I start up in the night, so convinced catastrophe has struck, that I crawl downstairs to check the extractor fan is still fixed to the kitchen wall, or the hall mirror hasn't moved. Both have fallen down twice already.

'Nobody would live like this if they had a choice,' I tell Reg.

'You can choose to make a fresh start,' he says. 'Common sense is all you need.' Being a socialist, he has limitless faith in the power of nurture over nature, and yet, he's watched me take out my tool box. He's seen the harm I can do, to myself and any solid matter that stands in my path.

Laziness and strength don't come into it, believe me; I can heave and graft with the best of them. When I was a student I was never out of dungarees in the vacation. As a labourer I was A1. My troubles started when my bosses tried to promote me to higher things. When I worked in the lollipop room at the sweet factory, they upgraded me to charge hand, gave me a white coat with a little metal badge. My responsibilities included supervision of the 'cow'. This was an automatic device with metal udders, suspended over the conveyor belt; it squirted fruit mixture into the lolly moulds as they rattled underneath; every so often it squirted too much, too little, or forgot to squirt at all. The girls on the conveyor would then shout 'Hold it' at the charge hand, and never seemed to tire of giving the phrase a double meaning. At this point it was my job to stop the machine, crawl under the belt and make appropriate adjustments to the 'cow' with a special spanner.

The first time that cry of 'Hold it' went up coincided with a visit from the under-manager. He was doing a quality check on the lollies, a batch of raspberry that particular morning. I stopped the machine, ducked under the belt, made my adjustments and smiled at him, waving my special spanner. Chaps together in a chaps' world. He returned the smile, re-started the machine, crawled across and stood by me, signifying his approval—reinforcement, we used to call it in the classroom. A lolly mould jolted merrily up the conveyor and rattled under the 'cow'. Streams of raspberry mixture shot out of the udders with such force that they cascaded over the mould and drenched both of us in a sticky, viscous mess. 'Hold it,' bawled the girls again, and one of them rushed across to stop the machine; but not soon enough to prevent another mould from rattling under the 'cow', and giving us a second drench.

The under-manager didn't move. A full minute he must've stood there, motionless, studying me through a thick veil of raspberry, so still and quiet, the girls forgot to giggle. Then he leaned forward and unpinned my little metal badge. 'You stupid berk,' he said, simply. The girl who'd stopped the machine crawled across and relieved me of my spanner. 'Clockwise,' she whispered, then she re-adjusted the 'cow' and re-started the machine. The udders functioned perfectly. 'Clockwise,' repeated the under-manager, and trailed off to the executive loo dripping raspberry. We both had red tints in our hair for days afterwards . . . At dinner break the clockwise girl sat next to me in the canteen.

'I pity the poor girl *you* marry,' she said.

'What I need is someone like you,' I said. 'How about it?' She examined me closely, obviously considering the proposition. She must have been all of sixteen.

'No,' she said, 'I like *my* men to be handy.'

Virility and handiness are inseparably linked in the popular imagination, as though there was no such thing as a eunuch craftsman. I don't expect you to believe this, but when I first got married I tried to hide the terrible truth from my wife. She was under the impression I was—well, a normal husband. This was the early 'seventies, don't forget, when role-swapping was still something actors did in long runs and matinees. We had a little basement flat in reasonable nick, so I got away with it for a while, painting the odd door or window frame, knocking in the odd nail when she wasn't within earshot; covering up or ignoring any repairs that required real tools. A kind but insensitive uncle had given me a well-stocked tool-box as a wedding present. 'A workman is only as good as his tools,' he said. It was like giving aspirins to a man with a broken neck . . . But the cover-up couldn't possibly last. Flats and houses aren't built that way. The kitchen tap started dripping, and quickly got worse. We used to eat most of our meals out there; she couldn't help but notice in the end, no matter how long I stood in front of it, or how loud I turned up the radio.

'I think the tap needs a new washer,' she said at last.

'Really?' said I. 'Are you sure?'

'See for yourself, you idiot. Can you fix it?' she asked.

'No problem,' I replied casually.

Buying a threepenny washer is not a task you can put off indefinitely. Within forty-eight hours destiny had caught up with me: I had opened the hated tool-box, taken a deep breath, seized a likely-looking wrench, offered up a prayer to my malevolent spirit, and advanced towards the weeping faucet with what I hoped was a confident swagger.

'Aren't you going to turn off the stop-cock first?' asked my wife.

'Of course,' I said, scornfully, and swaggered up the hall, hoping to God the comedian's friend was where it used to be in my parents' house. It was, under the floorboards by the front door. I returned to the tap, still swaggering, took a firm grip with the wrench, and wrenched. A bit stiff, a bit rusty, one of those old brass efforts. But I dismantled it down to the washer—which *did* look a little worn. Dismantled it, in no time at all, without shouting, swearing, sweating or stamping once.

'Surprise, surprise,' said my wife. 'I was beginning to think you were one of those.'

'One of those what?' I asked.

'Hopeless incompetents,' she said, and left me to my manly duties, having given me my first lesson in what mature relationships were all about. I didn't realise it at the time, mind you; I was too elated with my success at cheating the fates. I had put on a new washer in ten minutes flat: Orestes had kissed and made up with his Mum.

There was a bit of trouble when I came to put the tap

together again. It didn't seem to fit as well as it did before; a little cusp thing refused to stay in place. However, I wrenched everything into position, more or less, opened the stop-cock again, and rushed back into the kitchen to test my handiwork. The drip had gone, no problem, but when I turned the tap on, water spurted out of the top as well as the spout. I banged the tap irritably with my wrench, and discovered the spurt reduced to an ooze when I banged it upwards. Since I was working five days a week as a teacher and couldn't bang taps on a permanent basis, I lashed it to a nail above the sink, using a pyjama cord I took from the ironing basket. Rather ingenious, I thought, in the circumstances.

'We can't leave it like that,' said my wife.

'Just testing the flow,' I told her. 'We'll do the fine-tuning tomorrow.' She looked at me; a knowing look, profound, a Greek chorus kind of look. I brandished my wrench and swaggered off. Hubris, I think they call it.

I slept badly that night, my cordless pyjamas kept sliding round my ankles. When I crept out to the kitchen to make tea next morning—Sunday—I stepped into a largish sunken bath, fed by a graceful fountain issuing from the top of the tap. The stone floor was already six inches deep in water, seeping over the step into the living room. I backed up in horror—Noah's naughty neighbours must have reacted in much the same way, the morning the Ark was launched. But unlike them we were blessed with a stop-cock; I fled down the hall to shut it off. My unsecured pyjama trousers concertina'd round my knees, and brought me down with a crash to awaken the dead—my wife, that is, a very sound sleeper. Abandoning my trousers—and my reason—I turned off the water, hared back to the kitchen, waded across to the sink and began baling like a rum-soaked bosun, with the first thing that came to hand, a tea-pot—which I immediately smashed against the tap. My wife dragged herself as far as the living room doorway, and stared down at my bare hindquarters.

'Are you doing this for kicks, or is it a genuine emergency?' she asked.

'Phone a plumber,' I said, 'please . . .'

While I carried on baling, she tried half-a-dozen alleged twenty-four hour service numbers. Five plumbers in bed, and the sixth was at Mass but would come in an hour, God willing. In the course of that hour we were inundated again: a flood of enraged neighbours hammering at the door. It seemed that our stop-cock served the entire building, and we'd blighted their bath, breakfast, laundry and car-washing arrangements. An Englishman faced with an interruption to his Sunday routine is a terrible sight; I have seldom felt so rejected or so reviled. Conducting these angry interviews in my improvised baling kit didn't help, I suppose: an off-the-shoulder pyjama-top and a damp—rather revealing—tea-towel. Fortunately, the plumber turned out to be Irish and couldn't have been nicer.

'It's not your washer, it's your rose,' he said. 'The rose is worn away . . .' Poetry that, I thought so even at the time, standing beside him in my sodden tea-towel.

'I'm a great admirer of the Mahatma myself,' he said, as I showed him to the door. It took me a long time to work out what he meant. But, I ask you, 'the rose is worn away'—that wouldn't seem out of place in *Richard the Third*, or somewhere. Poetry and tragedy are inseparable, maybe, like virility and handiness.

After the rose had finally worn away, my wife laid an embargo on serious man-about-the-house stuff. To save face I told friends and relatives I had more important things to do, although I was always hard-pressed to make a convincing list of these activities. Explaining the lack of DIY in a man's life is harder than accounting for missing National Insurance stamps. Occasionally I dropped dark hints about some inherited disqualification, like haemophilia, say, but this upset the uncle who gave me the tool-box so much that I gave up the practice. Once in a while, when the strain of living in this nameless purdah became unbearable, I'd break out, in a wild, self-assertive frenzy, vaguely hoping I might burst through the incompetence barrier by brute force. For instance, I blasted a jagged hole in our back-door with a brace-and-bit and a chisel, to make a space for the cat-flap. I tell you, if I *had* been a haemophiliac, I wouldn't have survived that little lot. Another time I lobbied my wife so fiercely that she conceded a ready-made, 'easy-assemble' wooden shed ought to be within my capabilities —just—since we had a concrete strip already prepared. She had too much confidence in me. After three days wrestling round the lawn with thirty pieces of hut that wouldn't bolt together, we weren't looking at each other, let alone talking or sleeping. The smell of fresh timber still gives both of us a headache, and I daren't use cedar aftershave any more. In a desperate bid to save my marriage, I begged Reg to sort it out for me.

'You forgot to remove the protective packaging,' he said, pointing to some strips of wood and simply ripping them away. In an hour he had it up, and my two daughters were playing nurses and doctors inside. My wife felt the kids needed a name for these wild frenzies of mine—Daddyjobs, she called them. That is, any practical task involving excessive amounts of noise, sudden deathly silences and a rapid increase in marital tension. Reg tells me I ought to join a home-maintenance evening class. I haven't told *him* that I went along to enrol last year, and came over faint when I read the prospectus. Reg wouldn't understand.

DIY devotees are evangelicals, you see, fundamentalists. They believe that everybody and anybody can and must be converted to the one true religion; only ignorance, pride and original sin stand in the way. The one, true religion is, in fact, a primitive cult dedicated to the worship of Household Gods. These deities of hearth and threshold demand strict obedience, especially on Saturdays and Sundays. They seek the continuous improvement of all things domestic, and hold out the promise of an Ideal Home in a better place hereafter. Seriously, I know a pleasant, to all intents and purposes normal Penge couple who never stop decorating. Literally, Forth Bridge fashion. One room in the house is always under covers, cluttered up with ladders and buckets, reeking of paint and cellulose paste; every meal they eat seems to taste of turps. Only a deep sense of sin could keep them at it so constantly. I know Penge folk who mix pagan and Christian customs, like the early mediaeval Church. They cannot celebrate Christmas without the rites of DIY, nor Easter, nor Whitsun; and then there are the obligatory home improvements before and after the annual holiday. When Reg took me round the new home-care hypermarket in Penge, I thought it more like a temple than a shop: the size of it, the solemnity, the awe; long rows of altars, shrines and side-chapels crowded with consumer idols, before each of which little knots of the faithful paused reverently, and spoke in hushed voices; discussing how much they could afford when the offerings were taken up, I expect. 'You see how easy they make it for you nowadays,' said Reg, over and over again, as if he were telling the rosary. I was the only heathen in a communion of the chosen, and I realised I was damned. For me there was no salvation.

The realisation would have been hard to live with if it

hadn't been for old Jeff. He couldn't save me but he helped me survive, without intending to, of course. I tried to thank him once, and he obviously had no idea what I was talking about. Old Jeff is a handyman someone recommended to us. He has reduced the threat of Daddyjobs to a minimum, and improved the health of the family immeasurably. He's not cheap, but when you remember I get psychiatry and faith-healing for free, he's a bargain. I suppose he'd be in his mid-fifties, a tall, swarthy man in spotless white overalls. What you notice, though, is his permanent grin, the grin of a schoolboy who has just found a fifty-quid note. His power lies in his simplicity: Jeff is so handy he cannot conceive of anyone who is not—any man, I mean. Handiness is like air, everybody breathes it. For Jeff the world is no more than a collection of out-of-true uprights, angles and planes that will have to be dealt with in due course: squared-off, scribed-in, worked round, battened down. Jeff also believes in the fiction that I understand this world, but am too busy to deal with it personally, in spite of the fact that when he works for us, I spend most of my time making him tea and listening to tales of his exploits in much grander households. How he reversed a pair of oak doors here, or made some art-deco radiator covers there, or pieced together remnants of Jacobean panelling somewhere else. He'll draw you a ground plan of the job on the back of his cigarette packet; and an elevation on the inside of the lid. Then he'll light up and look at you for a few seconds, to make sure the scale of his achievement has been fully appreciated. At which point I'll shake my head in admiration, and purse my lips. 'Well, can't sit here chatting,' he'll say, and go back to fixing my dry-rot, as if he hadn't fixed it already, psychologically. Jeff wouldn't dream of discussing such mysteries with a woman, you see. He freely and unconditionally admits me into the brotherhood of handymen, and I—poor outcast that I am—cravenly suppress my pro-feminist good intentions, for the sheer pleasure of belonging, however briefly.

Nevertheless, it was old Jeff who set the scene for the final showdown.

'You need a roof aerial,' he said one day. He was fitting a new window in the sitting room, and trying to keep an eye on Wimbledon Fortnight at the same time. 'I can see six balls on that court,' he said. 'And Harry Carpenter's got three heads.'

'All right,' I told him, 'you can put an aerial up if you like.'

'That's no job for a handyman,' he said, proudly. 'Put it up yourself.'

'I suffer from vertigo, and the chimney stack's crumbling,' I lied.

'Put up a loft aerial, then—nothing to it.'

'Afraid I haven't got time, Jeff . . .'

'Forty minutes is all it takes.' His permanent grin had vanished, he was no longer the same, friendly old Jeff. I knew this was a challenge I couldn't avoid. I had to commit myself, or risk losing my associate membership of the brotherhood.

'Forty minutes,' I said. 'Oh well, no problem.'

'Forty minutes or less,' confirmed the spotty boy in the radio shop, 'no problem.'

'No problem?' shouted my wife. 'Remember the rose,' she added, poetically. I remembered. Poetry already, and the tragedy hadn't yet begun.

'I'm doing this on old Jeff's advice,' I lied; it was a bad habit I was getting into. She looked at me, her profound Greek chorus look, Cassandra to the life.

'Forty minutes,' she said. 'Shall we synchronise watches?'

I had the aerial up in the loft in forty-two and a half minutes exactly. I know, because my wife was shouting the zero-plus seconds at me through the trap-door. 'It's up,' I yelled back. And it was. Loose and a little askew, but *there*. No problem. The problem was finding a hole in the roof to run the cable through. For years I'd lain awake on rainy nights, worrying about leaks in that roof, listening for tell-tale drips, but could I find a hole in the right place when I wanted it? The loft began to tremble, as I orang-utanged around on the joists, clinging to the rafters with one hand, waving a flashlight with the other, the cable clenched between my teeth. I was soon smothered in dust, bits of lagging, and pigeons' mess.

'Are you all right?' called my wife. My reply was indistinct and unrepeatable. I'd finally worked out the cable would have to be pushed out under the eaves, and was worming my way into the acute angle where roof and joists meet, lying full-stretch, prodding the cable before me towards a narrow crack of daylight. But within a few seconds I was stuck fast, my outstretched fingers a good two feet from the crack. So then I speared the cable on a length of lath, and stabbed blindly at the daylight. The cable twisted and buckled like a live thing, and a cloud of eighty-year-old dust rose up, enveloping me completely. Coughing and choking, I rammed the cable towards the crack, as though I was fending off a rattlesnake, urging myself—and the telly serpent—on with a continuous stream of curses and groans. They must have been audible all the way along the avenue. I was suddenly reminded of Charles Bronson down the tunnel in *The Great Escape*, and I began to dramatise my efforts slightly, just in case it helped.

'What's wrong with Daddy?' I heard my daughters say.

'He's doing a Daddyjob,' came my wife's reply, 'go and watch television . . .'

The irony was transparent. It stirred me into a paroxysm of serpent prodding, until at last, through a storm of dust, I saw the end of the cable start to disappear through the eaves. Or so I thought.

I shinned down the ladder onto the landing, glissaded down the stairs, and out into the street. Action stations, phase two, operation aerial. (My wife had locked herself in the sitting room with the children.) I shaded my eyes and searched the eaves for signs of protruding cable. The retired railwayman three doors down was cleaning his car. He inspected my blackened face and matted clothes with interest.

'Having problems?' he asked.

'No problems,' I said grimly, and then I howled with rage. There was not an inch of cable to be seen anywhere.

'Hurt yourself?' asked the ex-railwayman sympathetically. I turned an anguished face on him.

'Don't pretend you care,' I hissed. 'Nobody cares . . .' In his surprise he emptied a bucket of dirty water down his gum-boots.

Out of the corner of my eye, I saw my wife—pale and angry—drawing the sitting room curtains, although it was barely three o'clock in the afternoon. But I had seen something else, too: a television cable snaking out from under the fascia board below the railwayman's eaves. In a flash it came to me: it was easier to push the cable *in* than pull it *out*; what a fool I was! With a whoop I charged back indoors, mounted the stairs four at a time, and leaped up the ladder in two bounds. A kind of nautical jolliness came over me as I began yanking in my cable. 'Yo-ho-ho,' I chanted . . . The trap-door into the loft suddenly closed with a crash, and I heard the sound of sobbing beneath it. I stopped yanking.

'What's up now?' I asked, unfairly. There was no answer, only incoherent, grown-up sobs.

Then a small voice: 'Mummy says she's running away.' And another small voice: 'We don't want a new aerial.'

'Tell Mummy I'm coming down.'

Two small voices answered in unison: 'She doesn't want you any more.' I threw away the cable and strode towards the trap-door, manfully, forgetting there were no floor-boards. As my foot sank into the soft mush of lagging between the joists, I reached out for a hand-hold to stop my leg thrusting straight through to the landing below. My fingers closed round the shaky, newly-erected aerial, and down it came, with a musical prang, like a tubular bell; one half on top of me, as I lay stretched across the joists, the other half puncturing the bedroom ceiling.

Late that night I removed my tool-box from the hall cupboard and put it in the back of our old Mini-traveller. I drove out to Keston Ponds, parked in a lay-by and carried the box down to the water's edge. A melon-slice of moon rose above the trees and lit a path across the still water. I raised the hated wedding present to my chest and heaved it away from me along the path. The box hit the surface with a great smack and disappeared at once, sending wave after wave up over my shoes and straight through to my socks. I turned and ran back to the car. Like a criminal, like Orestes. Driving home, however, I felt rather pleased with myself. The Fates had been putting the boot in for years; now they were getting a taste of their own medicine. I only hoped they wouldn't turn too nasty. After all, why should men submit to these outdated stereotypes? If it was all right for a woman to be an all-in wrestler or Prime Minister—or both if she chose—why wasn't it all right for me to be a domestic incompetent? After all, fair's fair: my cooking and ironing had come on a treat recently. I was just beginning to warm to this argument with myself when the police car flagged me down. A courting couple had seen me dispose of a heavy metal object. I tried to explain.

'What was in this tool-box?' they asked.

'Tools,' I told them.

'Old tools?'

'Nearly new, unused tools.' They couldn't accept this. It was easier to believe in safe-breaking or bomb-making equipment. 'How are you on Greek tragedy?' I asked. They looked at me: they looked at each other. 'Forget that,' I said, 'send for a frogman. Better still, telephone my wife, she'll tell you.' Then I had second thoughts. 'If you're offering,' I said, 'I wouldn't mind a cell for the night.'

10 *Penge Agonistes*

'Penge Neglected,' said the headline in a local paper the other week. They were discussing the social services, and they had a point, but I'm not sure it doesn't go deeper than that. Nothing good ever came out of Penge—I'm told that's a proverb in places like Chislehurst and Green Street Green. If so, there's no justification for it. Proverbs grow: this one was implanted.

A hundred and fifty years ago Penge was an unremarkable, pleasant little village that might have attracted the notice of invalids, health freaks and other visitors, taking the waters on Beulah Hill, or down at Sydenham Wells—George the Third, for example. Although illness was likely to disorientate the poor man, and there were those who said he never knew where he was—Penge or Prague, it was all the same to him. However, when the Great Exhibition was re-assembled just down the road, everything changed for Penge; suddenly, we were at the centre of national life. Royal visits, military tattoos, concerts, competitions, displays, balloon ascents, airships, motor trials, sports of all kinds. We had Cup-Finals at the Crystal Palace before Wembley was even thought of—eighty years of spectacle. Nobody made jokes or rude remarks about Penge in those days, but those days are gone. They vanished over-night. The Big Fire of 1936 not only removed Paxton's Palace from the centre of things, it erased Penge and its neighbours from the national memory, too. The sparks that showered down upon the High Street that night were a farewell salute. The real Penge faded away, and a comic phantom slowly re-emerged in its place, like a mangy Cheshire cat, one of a litter that the English keep for their private amusement—places chosen for their (assumed) insignificance, for the reassurance they give to almost anyone living almost anywhere else. The inference being that both they and it are bound to be superior. An accident, a spectacular accident, robbed us of our identity in the space of a few hours, and gave us a red nose instead.

A touching scenario, and I don't believe a word of it. Too pat, too tidy—reversals don't happen as neatly as that in the real world. I suspect a conspiracy, a national conspiracy, although I wouldn't rule out international involvement. A conspiracy against *Penge*, I'm talking about. Suppose—wait for it now—what if the burning of the Palace was merely a cover for the relegation of Penge? A masterly cover, I grant you, a spectacular one. To this day, nobody knows how the fire started, or nobody will admit to knowing; and yet that was the biggest single fire London has ever seen. For pyrotechnics it beat anything Mr Charles Brock laid on in the Palace grounds. There were more people at that blaze than there had been at regular, organised functions. I find that odd, very fishy. My contention is that it *was* organised, the whole boiling. Somebody, lots of somebodies, perhaps, wanted Penge tucked quietly out of the way. Now—you don't have to tell me—why? This is the question you're asking yourselves. Penge? you snigger, a conspiracy against—? And you choke on the name, or pronounce it the French way, to emphasise your point. Well, I can provide an answer to that question. Very likely you won't be convinced by it; I'm the first to agree that we unwaged, fulltime professional observers—and amateur househusbands—are prone to exaggeration, occasionally. It's a professional hazard. But hyperbole stretches the mind as well as the facts; my hogwash can do you no harm in small doses, if you've read this far, if it *is* hogwash.

People flocked from miles around to see that building go up in flames, all kinds of people; one of them was Winston Churchill—it's a matter of historical fact. The story goes, he stopped off on his way home to Chartwell from the Commons. I don't believe it. That man never stopped off anywhere, every puff of cigar had a serious political purpose. As he watched the fire, he was recorded as saying—and he said it more than once—'This is the end of an age.' Most commentators have assumed he was referring to the Victorian age, or the Industrial Revolution, or even the Empire, although I don't suppose anyone asked him exactly what he meant at the time; Churchillian oratory wasn't designed to be interrupted. 'This is the end of an age.' Now, I put it to you, that what he actually said, in an unguarded moment, was: 'This is Penge's new page'—a dangerous leak that could have become a torrent, if a smart press officer hadn't spotted the gaffe, and scrambled it. You will quite rightly object that there is no record of the great man referring to Penge on any other occasion. My friend Reg never tires of telling me this, and he's no admirer of the great man.

'Don't you start messing about with history,' he tells me. 'It's bad enough as it is.'

'History is meant to be messed about with,' I say, 'that's how it happens.'

'Show me,' he says, 'come on, show me a single mention of Penge in Churchill's books, his speeches, in Hansard, anywhere. I doubt if he even knew of its existence.'

'That's suspicious in itself,' I say, 'the omission cries

out for investigation. It was obviously planned,' I tell him. 'The neglect of Penge has a serious political purpose. It always had, and it always will, unless we expose it.'

'You should never have read that book on lateral thinking,' says Reg. 'You can't think straight any more.' Coming from Reg, this is a compliment.

'Churchill said, "This is Penge's new page",' I repeat, 'and he meant it.'

'How could he mean it?' asks Reg. 'It doesn't mean anything.'

'The meaning is there, only you refuse to accept it,' I tell him.

'Don't go on,' he says. But I always do.

As I see it—and to simplify, of course—before the Big Fire, or BF as we call it here, you couldn't take a walk round Penge without tripping over some prominent, public figure: W.G. Grace, Ernest Shackleton, Fitzroy of the *Bounty,* Viscount Falkland. They lived in these parts without difficulty or embarrassment—cricketers, explorers and Navy men—you can't get more public or prominent in England than that. Post-BF, public and prominent figures shun the place; it's as though their union had blacked us, and set up pickets. I don't believe in coincidence on that sort of scale. *Somebody* has warned the public and prominent to stay away, and *Somebody* leans on them if they try to buck the trend. Paranoiac I may be, but the facts speak for themselves . . . A famous television entertainer came to live amongst us. Continually in the news, he was, and seemingly, not ashamed to acknowledge his residence in the press or before the cameras. What happened? Within three years of setting up house in a no-go area, his very successful career went on the blink; there wasn't a variety producer or chat show host that would engage him. He was reduced to playing number two tours of the Far East, and British Council cabarets, simply in order to keep his daughters at Roedean.

It was the same with the up-and-coming rock singer; he took a flat just around the corner. Stable young lad: a couple of reasonably successful singles, an album and three appearances on *Top of the Pops* seemed to make very little difference to his life-style, apart from a second-hand Mercedes and a faster turnover of girlfriends. I used to bump into him at the baker's, and actually spoke to him once.

'Penge won't be able to hold you much longer,' I said to him.

'Don't you believe it,' he said, 'you need roots in the music game. My next album is called *South East Twenty* . . .'

By the time that record was released he'd gone off on a long American tour—*Absent Friends* was the title they printed on the sleeve—and neither album nor singer was ever heard of again. Some say the boy changed his name; I wouldn't know, he certainly changed his address. The local author who was nominated for a national literary prize moved house even before the jury announced their verdict—not that it did him much good. He also changed his name a little later, but I think that was something to do with writing scripts for a soap-opera. Impoverished, literary excellence is a tradition we cherish in England, and he was a sensitive, conservative soul.

Anyhow, I think I've made my point: Penge is officially off-limits to anyone in the public eye—even a mote in its eye. There was a crooked estate agent who made a million swindling simple Pengeians, yet he lived here quite happily for years, until he began driving around in a white Rolls with a personalised number plate, and indulging in a taste for litigation. He's doing time now, and Pengeians are swindled by a discreeter class of crook. The only exception to my rule is a senior journalist on *The Times*, who can be seen smiling at his own articles three or four mornings a week on Penge East station. However, I notice he is careful to use initials rather than a Christian name in his by-line. And there are those who maintain a staff job on *The Times* is itself a guarantee of anonymity; old and trusted retainers of the establishment are heard but not seen, disappearing quietly below stairs between editions.

Anonymity is what modern Penge was created to provide. Not for the aboriginals: they are only there as background, local colour; they are only there for the benefit of a privileged few. I first became aware of this elite when my wife returned to fulltime work. Neighbourhood colleagues began to invite her to dinner parties, and I went along as consort. An unwaged househusband with no special interests, I spent long evenings in draughty corners soaking up free booze, and listening to other wallflowers. After several of these sessions I became aware that a good percentage of the wallflowers were civil servants, with unspecified but highly confidential jobs. What a boring old fart, I'd think. 'How interesting.' I'd say. 'Which ministry do you work for?' 'Defence,' would come the answer. Or 'Foreign Office', perhaps. 'May one ask what you do?' I'd say. 'You can ask but I can't tell you,' would come the reply. Then they'd launch into an account of a visit to their old public school, or Lord's, or Twickenham, or occasionally a regimental reunion. Quick as a flash, I'd ask them their former rank, and whether their work was Intelligence. Then they'd say: 'Not exactly,' and tell me about their roses, or their sunflowers, and what to do about slugs. As a conversational long-stop they tended to favour opera. Most of them were bachelors with old, ailing mothers in remote parts of the country. If I asked them why they were living in an unlikely place like Penge, they answered that it was convenient. 'Convenient for what?' I'd say, and they'd shrug, offer to fetch me another drink, and forget to come back.

There was no sudden moment of insight: the terrible truth filtered into my mind very slowly, like a lavatory cistern re-filling. I hardly dare to put it down in black and white, even now. My native Penge is obviously a dormitory suburb for middle-ranking officers in the Security Service. Of course, I can't prove it, but everything fits. British Intelligence expanded rapidly in the run-up to the War. They had urgent need of a 'safe' billeting area for the vastly increased numbers of staff, a convenient shadow into which they could slip, after a hard day's defence of the realm; somewhere close to Whitehall but way beyond suspicion; somewhere an enemy would never dream of looking. Since no such place existed, they decided to invent it, or rather re-create it, like the phoenix, out of the funeral pyre of Paxton's Palace. Ever since the night of the Big Fire, the face of national security has hidden itself in off-duty hours behind the comic mask of Penge: this was 'Penge's new page', as Sir Winston inadvertently said on that fateful night . . . Well, it's an interesting *theory*, you have to admit. Far fetched, of course. But remember, MI5 and MI6 got big by not being obvious.

When I first confided the theory to Reg, he was perfectly frank, so to speak. 'Unemployment has finally blown your mind,' he said. *I* said it was only a theory, I didn't necessarily believe it either; it was part of a continuing socratic dialogue I was having with myself. After all, Penge needed explaining somehow. Reg said that if that was what university did for you, he was glad he never stayed on at school. He blamed the arts faculty entirely. I reminded him that Penge already had a local espionage connection: Joyce lived on the other side of the hill before the War.

'Rubbish,' said Reg, 'he was in Zurich.'

'Not the *Finnegan's Wake* one,' I said: 'William Lord Haw-Haw, the spy, the one who did propaganda broadcasts for the Germans.' Reg was almost beside himself.

'Are you now going to tell me that Penge was a base for Goebbels and the Gestapo as well?' I looked at him.

'Reg, that's brilliant. Now you're getting the idea.' He grabbed at my arm angrily.

'OK you daft sod, we'll play it your way, and I'm warning you, I may belong to the hard Left, but I'm a patriot—my country right or wrong. If you breathe one word of this cobblers to me ever again, I'll spill the beans to Sir Antony Duff in person.' I thought about it.

'He could give me a job, you need imagination in MI5,' I said.

'A job?' said Reg. 'He'll have you embalmed in concrete and dropped in Surrey Docks.' I stared at him.

'Maybe that's why I can't get a job now,' I said. 'He's put me on a proscribed list.' Reg stared at *me*.

'And the millions of others out of work?' he asked. 'Are you blaming MI5 for that, too?' I agreed it didn't seem likely. But millions of unemployed hadn't seemed very likely a few years ago; there had to be an explanation for everything. Reg started on a long lecture about monetarism and the shift to the Right. I interrupted him, gently.

'Suppose,' I said, 'just suppose it was *James* Joyce—not William—who used to live on the other side of the hill?' Reg got up and walked out of the room. Without looking at me.

Epilogue

My friend Reg finds my obsession with the Penge phenomenon boring, as you may have gathered. 'Allusive, whimsy, escapist flim-flam,' he says. 'That stuff went out with Belloc and Chesterton.' Reg makes his five School Certs go a long way—on the whole, he's wasted at the Lewisham Gas Board.

'You've lost touch with political reality,' he tells me. I protest that I looked after the kids when my wife and his went down to Greenham Common for a week. 'You were only obeying orders,' says Reg. 'Unemployment has corroded your political will.' I remind him that oxidisation set in a good while before I joined the multitudes of the unemployed. As an idealistic student I stood shoulder to shoulder with him at the Grosvenor Square anti-Vietnam rally, and suffered a deeply traumatic experience: a large apple core aimed at a mounted policeman fell short and hit me in the eye, causing an instant political catalepsy. 'More whimsy,' cries Reg.

'Not at all,' I say, 'It was a Winter Pearmain and it left me with a detached retina.' The world has never looked quite the same since. But it became very clear to me that violent protest might be the end to the means, and that putting the same old boot on someone else's big foot was no way to prevent a kick in the crutch.

'Aphorisms are the last resort of the scoundrel,' replies Reg.

'Can I quote you?' I ask him.

He's entitled to his opinion. I *am* a capitalist jackal, I suppose, although I understand the jackal is actually a very sociable, co-operative creature. I spend my days muddling away at househusbandry, unwaged, unnoticed, unprotesting; idly speculating on the jetsam washed up on London's southern shoreline. I'm like one of those archaeologists who poke around in mediaeval middens. Posterity always gets the truest, most intimate picture of the past from its left-overs and leavings. Government buildings, law courts, cathedrals, air-bases, roads and factories are monuments to our self-deception in the end. It's the rub, smudge, grease and bellyache of dull, domestic living that will provide our final testament, a few centuries from now. That's a comfort—bit of a laugh really, in a century four fifths over that could still be our last . . . I sit here peering into the Penge midden as it piles up around me, like one of those old Romanies who used to live on Gipsy Hill, hoping the slops and lees will tell all, before it's too late. If I come across anything interesting, I'll let you know, but I wouldn't depend on it. On the other hand, these confessions may be of some use to midden-rakers yet to come; if they ever manage to find them amongst all the other rubbish.